YOUTH • WORK • PRESS

Published by

NATIONAL YOUTH AGENCY

17-23 Albion Street, Leicester LE1 6GD.
Tel: 0116.285.3700. Fax: 0116.285.3777.
E-mail: nya@nya.org.uk
Internet: www.nya.org.uk

ISBN 0 86155 261 X

£12.95

Editor/Designer: Denise Duncan

YOUTH · WORK · PRESS

is the publishing imprint of the National Youth Agency

CONTENTS

ENDINGS

ACKNOWLEDGMENTS/CONTRIBUTORS

With many thanks to

Zoey Caldwell, Ann McKay, Ingrid Davies, Nicky Hardwick, Ben Carr and Lorraine Clark (Young Citizens Project, North), Charlotte Rogers, Jeanette Williams (Young Citizens Project; South), Anie Twigg (Hertfordshire Careers Service Ltd), Deborah Morgan and Kevin Stewart (HCC Youth Offending Team, North Herts), Gillian Porter (QE11), Tony Hunt (HCC Learning Services), Sophie and Toby Oakes-Rogers (Mill Mead School), Martin Cooke and Mary Westgate (HCC Youth Service) and Deborah Mulroney (HCC Education Department).

Thanks also to any youth workers not mentioned who have been a part of the projects that are referred to.

ABOUT THE AUTHOR

Vanessa Rogers is a qualified youth worker with a masters degree in Community Education and over 10 years experience within the Hertfordshire Youth Service both at practitioner and management levels. She has gained extensive experience managing a large youth centre, developing detached projects and working directly with young people in urban and rural areas. Currently employed within the Hertfordshire Youth Justice Service, Vanessa uses her youth work skills to develop creative strategies to engage with young people at risk of offending or disaffection. She is also the author of *Have You Ever . . . ?* (a resource handbook for detached workers), *Lets Talk Relationships . . .* and *So You Want to Work with Young People?* (a resource for training and supporting volunteer workers) all published by the National Youth Agency.

INTRODUCTION

This diverse collection of activities, worksheets and team-building games has been put together as a response to the increased demand to work with young people who are below the traditional youth service target age group. Other professionals, such as social workers, Connexions advisers, YOT workers and voluntary sector projects have also contributed with ideas that are effective and enjoyable.

The aim of this handbook is to engage with children and young people aged 9 to 13 who may not take up statutory services, but who could respond to a youth work approach.

Many of the issues identified for this younger group, both nationally and at community level, are familiar to youth workers working with older teenagers; young people hanging around on street corners, difficulties experienced with peer relationships and bullying, educational under achievement and low self-esteem. The main problem is that these difficulties are now surfacing in this younger group.

With the introduction of the 1998 Crime and Disorder Act and the setting up of Youth Offending Teams (YOTs) across the country, many local authorities are keen to take on the new Government directive of early intervention and prevention. The focus on young people aged 9 to 13 who are at risk of offending or disaffection is increasing as a response to new laws. This is especially important to ensure that as many young people are diverted away from entering the criminal justice system as possible.

This resource book has been devised to support young people in working through some of the issues that are important to them. Most activities can be used for individual or group work, as appropriate.

MAKING THE RULES

These 'rules' set the scene for any programme of work and encourage children to explore their expectations and consider ways to make sessions as successful as possible. The action plan supports the young people in setting their own goals.

WARM-UPS

These warm-up games or icebreakers are a good way to start a session and encourage children and young people to start to work together.

GETTING TO KNOW EACH OTHER

The worksheets and activities contained in this section enable children and young people to start considering the people and things that are important to them. These can be positive and negative experiences and you need to be sure that the young person is clear about the boundaries of your confidentiality and at what stage you will need to pass information on.

These sessions also offer the opportunity for workers to stress that working together is on a voluntary basis and is not a punishment because people think they are 'bad children' or have been 'naughty'. It is a good time to reassure young people about your role, and encourage them to identify positive outcomes for themselves. Building a positive relationship now is important to the success of future work.

EXPRESSING YOURSELF

This section focuses on supporting young people in recognising and expressing their feelings. This includes ways to recognise how others are feeling and encourages empathy and understanding.

The base line for all the sessions is the recognition that everyone has a wide range of feelings and emotions that are a response to both internal and external factors. This includes emotions such as love and happiness, as well as fear and anger, and it underlines the right to feel these. Some sessions focus on specific feelings and what their personal 'triggers' are,

The activities encourage young people to look at different ways of expressing themselves and to reflect on what motivates them.

MAKING FRIENDS

Peer relationships and friendships are very important to young people. This chapter contains activities and worksheets that explore the impact and value of these. It encourages young people to look at what they can offer a prospective friend and considers the issues of trust, honesty and reciprocity.

Working together and positive play are the strands running through all the games and teambuilding activities. These encourage young people to develop skills to share resources with others, support friends through a task and to realise what can be achieved by working together.

The sessions support children in considering the things that contribute to both positive and negative relationships and how they can effect change. This includes peer pressure and encourages the ability to say 'no'. Young people are encouraged to think through their actions and the consequences of decisions are considered.

ENDINGS

The activities suggested in this final section aim to close group or individual sessions on a positive note. They offer feedback for workers to consider the success of the programme, and offer chances for the children to reflect on what they have just participated in.

MAKING THE RULES

1 PARENT/GUARDIAN CONSENT

It is good practice to obtain a consent form for work with all young people, but if you are starting a piece of work with a child under 13 it is vital. Consent needs to be given by whoever has parental responsibility for the young person. This can be a parent, but could be another relative such as a grandparent, or foster carer or a named social worker. Whoever it is, make sure that they have signed the form and given you as much information as possible before you start.

The consent form should clearly state who you are, what the aims of the sessions are and where they will be held. It is also important to gain some knowledge about any medication that may be needed during the young person's time with you. As well as medication needed during the session, such as an inhaler for asthma, it is also useful to know if a child has regular treatment for a condition, such as Ritalin for ADHD. All of this will inform the sessions that you plan.

Finally, make sure that you have a contact number you can reach while the sessions are on in the event of an emergency. Then, if there is an accident or a problem later you have the information to hand to support the young people.

EXPLAINING THE NEED

Lots of people are put off contact with agencies if they think that there is lots of paperwork or form filling involved. It is important to explain to the young person and their family why you are asking for consent.

If you are planning a home visit to meet with the young person and their family prior to starting any work, you could take the consent form with you. This offers the opportunity to explain fully what it is you are going to be doing and encourages both the child and parent/carer to ask any questions they may have.

You can also make sure that any expectations are realistic on both sides. For example, if a young person has been refusing to go to school for several months it is unlikely they will go the next day just because you have visited!

By having these discussions now parents, carers and young people can make informed choices as to whether they choose to take part or not.

ANTI-OPPRESSIVE PRACTICE

To ensure that you can meet the needs of the young people you are planning to work with it is a good idea to consider what barriers there may be to accessing your provision.

For some young people you will need to consider their cultural or religious background and decide if the work you are hoping to do will meet their needs. For example, will the family be comfortable with where you are planning to meet? Would the young person be happier working with someone of the same religion? If you think there may be problems consult with the young people and their family in advance to discuss and agree options.

Consider gender issues and if appropriate offer the option of a same sex worker. This can be especially important if the child has a history of bad relationships with a particular gender, or is known to social services as a child protection case.

Make sure that the building and space you plan to work in is appropriate for the young person. Most new buildings have good access for wheelchair users, but older buildings can be more difficult to get into. Similarly facilities, such as toilets, need to be suitable.

As well as physical disabilities consider children you may be working with who have conduct disorders or who are liable to 'run' at some point during the work. Good pointers to the suitability of a building are things like:

1 Is the area clear so that the children can run and play without tripping or damaging anything?
2 Does the building face straight onto a main road? What precautions can you take?
3 Have you agreed an action plan with the parents/carers and your co-worker in the event of a young person running off?

All these issues can be discussed beforehand and agreements copied and sent to everyone. Additionally, you may want to do a risk assessment for particular activities.

DURING THE SESSION

Either you or your co-worker should assume responsibility for holding consent forms for the duration of the session. If you plan a block of sessions for a project, put all the dates and details on the consent form, so it only has to go home once for signing.

After the project the consent forms can be filed with your evaluation sheets.

2 CONSENT FORM

Worker's name .... Date .... / .... / ....
Contact number ....

The aim of meeting is to ....
....
....
....
Dates; .... / .... / ...., ... / .... / ...., ... / .... / ....
Time .... Venue ....

I give consent for .... **(name of young person) to be allowed to take part in this project and to participate in the activities involved.**

I understand these will include sessions that look at;

- **developing interpersonal skills;**
- **anti-social behaviour and taking consequences of actions;**
- **managing anger and expressing feelings;**
- **teambuilding and groupwork;**
- **building self-confidence and raising self-esteem; and**
- **peer pressure and bullying.**

Medical conditions

Has .... any medical conditions that may need treatment during a session? Yes/No.
If 'yes', please give details
....
....
Have they any known allergies?
....
Last immunisation against tetanus? ....
National Health Service Medical Card Number ....
Is there any other information, which you believe we should know?
....
Do you give consent for emergency medical treatment if necessary? Yes/No
....

Signature ....
(Parent or guardian)

Date .... / .... / ....

Address and telephone number

....

....

....

....

....

....

If you have any queries or would like to discuss anything further please contact me on the above number.

3 GROUP RULES

It is a good idea to start work with any group by agreeing some ground rules or a contract that everyone signs up to. Group rules are not the same as the non-negotiable rules or regulations that are either statutory or set by management committees. These tend to be around health and safety or legal requirements, such as child protection procedures. Make sure that both workers and young people are aware of the difference and know the boundaries to your confidentiality.

Good group rules include ways that young people and workers can work together to enjoy sessions and create a safe and supportive environment. Group rules provide the boundaries so that everyone can learn effectively together, but also provide opportunities for the whole group to participate in something that has a clear outcome.

It can be a difficult process to engage young people who have only just come together, but a contract needs to be facilitated at an early stage in the life of the group. Spending time looking at the things that really matter to the young people is a worthwhile task, even if it does seem extremely hard work at times! With younger children and young people you may need to be more creative to get a good response.

Youth workers should participate in the process but not take over with their own rules. The point is to create a framework that everyone is happy with and feels comfortable working within.

Young people should be supported in considering the following:

- **everyone joins the group bringing different life experiences and values;**
- **if the group is to be effective everyone needs the opportunity to take part and be heard;**
- **the group is a safe place to experiment with new ideas and activities and to make a mistake is okay; and**
- **what happens within the group stays within it, apart from child protection issues.**

If new members join the group you will need to review the group rules to make sure that any needs or ideas they have are considered. Similarly new workers will need to agree to the contract.

The following ideas are specifically for younger children although you could adapt them to work with those aged over 13. They take into account different levels of understanding and ability and are fun as well as productive!

4 GROUP GRAFFITI WALL

This is good fun, but you will need to assess the children or young people's literacy skills to make sure they are not going to feel daunted by the task.

Aim: To produce a set of Group Rules that everyone has contributed to.

YOU WILL NEED

- A large wall
- Flipchart sheets
- Marker pens

HOW TO DO IT

Cover two separate areas of wall with flipchart paper and lay out a good selection of marker pens before the young people arrive.

Divide the group into two and explain the task and importance of developing a group contract.

If you think that the young people may need some prompts to be able to do this, write some questions to stimulate thoughts on the graffiti sheets in advance.

For example

✔ **What would make this group good for you?**

✔ **How do you like people to talk to you?**

✔ **What will you do to make this group a success?**

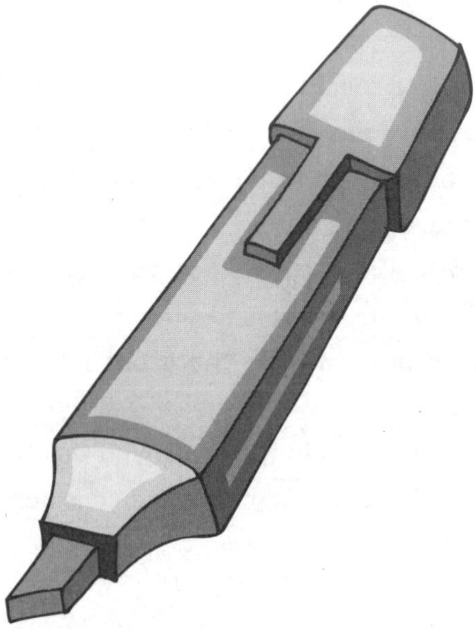

Once everyone is clear what is required of them show them the pens - and stand well back!

Explain that no-one has the right to alter or erase someone else's comments - there will be space to challenge and reach agreement at the end. If they see anything they especially agree with ask them to put a tick by the comment or word.

Ensure that everybody has a go at expressing themselves and that no-one takes over the wall.

Once the space has been filled ask the group to stand back and review what they have produced. Are there common themes? How many ticks are there? Does anyone want to talk about what they have written or ask about anything put on the wall?

Pull out the main themes from both sheets and agree a set of group rules that incorporates everybody's ideas. This can be written up onto another sheet.

Finally, take up the pens again and ask each member of the group (including staff) to sign and date the contract. Display during group times as a reminder of agreements made.

5 INDIVIDUAL CONTRACTS

Contracts tend to be associated with group work, but it is a good place to start when you are planning to work individually with a child or young person too. The process allows space for the young person to question why they are with you and express what they would like to achieve.

Aim: The point of this session is to gain an understanding from the young person of what they see as their concerns and issues and what they hope to gain from a contract with you.

YOU WILL NEED

- A copy of the CONTRACT CIRCLE
- Pens

HOW TO DO IT

Introduce the idea that to make the sessions really useful to the young person you need to identify areas that they would like to work on with you. Encourage them to take ownership of the contract so that it becomes a useful piece of work, not something imposed upon them.

Suggest that this contract is a two-way process that looks at what you will do to make the sessions productive, and identifies the young person's responsibilities to the process.

Hand out a copy of the CONTRACT CIRCLE. Use the headings to prompt discussion and support the child in identifying achievable goals. Use the contract to review progress in later meetings.

CONTRACT CIRCLE

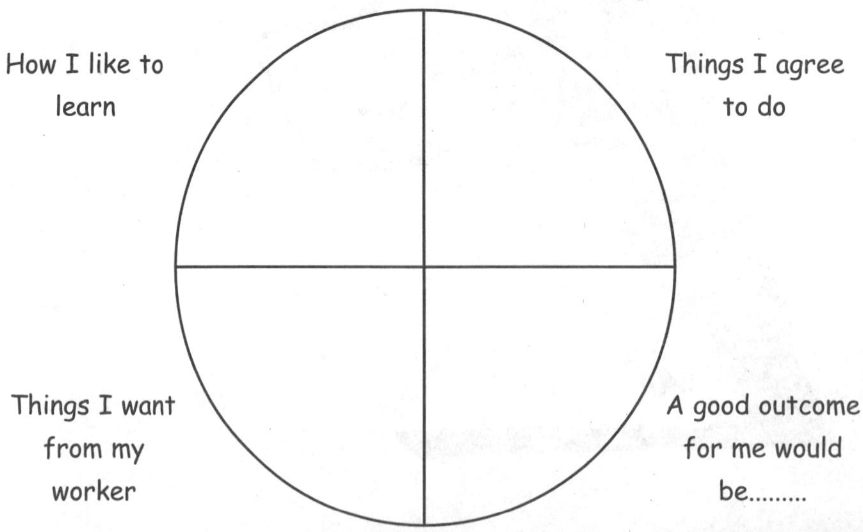

6 MY ACTION PLAN

Action plans enable children and young people to focus on areas that they would like to work on. These can be personal goals, such as learning a new skill, or can be part of a specific programme, for example, looking at anger management or offending behaviour.

Aim: To engage children in the decision-making process of how they spend their time in sessions with you.

YOU WILL NEED

- Pens
- A copy of the ACTION PLAN sheet

HOW TO DO IT

Make sure that you set aside time when you can work through the action plan process with the young person quietly.

Explain that the point of this session is to devise an action plan that belongs to them. Spend time reassuring the child that this is not a list of things that other people think is 'wrong' with them, but a chance to spend time concentrating on goals that are important to them. It is also the opportunity to explain the boundaries of your confidentiality and who else you intend to share information with.

Hand out a copy of the ACTION PLAN sheet and a selection of pens. Encourage the child to personalise the sheet in any way they want to - for example, colouring in the spaces, or drawing pictures of things important to them.

Now, support the young person in completing the sheet. Encourage them to set themselves specific, realistic goals so that they do not become disappointed or disinterested in the first week. For example, rather than 'I will never get into trouble at school ever again', might be more achievable if it reads 'I will use the "time out" system in class, rather than walking out of school'.

Stress that this action plan is not about 'failing', but is about personal goals and achievements. Make sure that the young person can see the personal benefits to any goal reached by considering 'celebrations' of targets met.

Finally, this action plan is intended as a working document, so it can be revised or updated at any time. Explain to the child that it is not a set-in-stone plan. Build in review dates so that you can see if goals are being achieved and when a new action plan is needed.

MY ACTION PLAN

This is your action plan to look at the things that are important to you. Choose things that you would like to work on. Be realistic and focus on things that you think you can do and remember to celebrate your successes!

What do I hope to achieve?

....

....

How could I do it?

....

....

What support would I like?

....

....

How long will it take?

....

....

How will I know if I have been successful?

....

....

What could stop me?

....

....

How will I celebrate my achievements?

....

....

My name .... **Date** .... / .... / ....

WARM-UPS

7 FIZZ-BUZZ

This game encourages children and young people to listen and offer each other support. It is a good warm-up exercise and should be played at a fast pace in a place where you can make lots of noise!

Aim: To remember what has been said and crack the Fizz-Buzz code!

YOU WILL NEED

- Nothing

HOW TO DO IT

Choose a leader and ask the rest of the group to form a wide circle facing each other.

With the facilitator's support the leader decides what the 'code' is going to be. Make sure you consider what levels of numeracy there are within the group and encourage the leader to choose appropriately. For example, **numbers divisible by 2 (e.g. 2, 4, 6, 8 etc)**. 2 then becomes Fizz, and the leader chooses another multiple to be Buzz, e.g. 4. Fizz-Buzz is any number that is divisible by both 2 and 4, e.g. 8, 12 etc.

Explain to the group that the aim of the game is to crack the secret Fizz-Buzz code. With younger children it is best to facilitate the start of the game by going around the circle and giving each person a number to demonstrate what you are asking as well. **So, 1, Fizz, 3, Buzz, 5, 6, 7, Fizz-Buzz, 9, Fizz etc . . .**

Allow young people time to think but try and keep the pace going. If someone says Fizz or Buzz in the wrong place they are 'out'. The last person in wins!

8 STORM

The more young people taking part in this group warm-up the more effective the 'storm' they create! This is a great invitation for them to be as loud as they can!

Aim: The idea is for the group to produce the sounds of a storm. It is a good introduction to group work as it will only happen if they work together to create the effect.

YOU WILL NEED

- Nothing

HOW TO DO IT

Invite the young people to form a circle large enough so that everyone can see each other. Explain that together you are going to create a 'storm' with sound.

The group facilitator then begins by slowly rubbing both hands together and motions for the rest of the group to join in.

Once the whole group is rubbing hands, the leader then begins to click their fingers, encouraging the others to follow. By this point the young people will have got the idea that they should follow whatever action the leader does.

As the noise of the finger clicking rises, change the clicking to clapping. Encourage the group to be as loud as possible!!! Finally bring the noise up to a crescendo by additionally stamping feet while continuing clapping. Allow the full effect of the storm to be felt for a minute or so.

As the storm rages slowly stop stamping your feet. As the young people follow begin to gradually halt the movements in reverse, allowing space for each stage.

Bring the noise back down to hand rubbing only and then slowly end.

9 INTRODUCTION CIRCLE

This form of introduction works well with all ages, but for the best effect you need plenty of space to sit down and spread out a bit.

Aim: To introduce the group to each other and the youth workers.

YOU WILL NEED

- A ball of brightly coloured string or wool

HOW TO DO IT

Make a large circle, placing the youth workers apart within the group.

Keeping a hold of one end, the person holding the string throws it to another member of the group to welcome them and introduce themselves. For example: 'Welcome to the group, my name is Krishna.' The second person then replies: 'Welcome Krishna, my name is Jamie' and throws it to the next member. This continues until each person has been welcomed and introduced. You may want to make some ground rules about this with the group before you start so that no-one gets left out.

As the exercise progresses you will begin to see a web forming. This is a visualisation of the process. Be really sensitive here to anyone who looks like they are feeling excluded. Ask the young people to look at and reflect on the web they have made.

Finally, ask the young people to put the string down in front of them onto the ground and step away. From this you can all see the interaction of the group.

10 DUCK, DUCK, GOOSE!

This is another energetic warm-up activity so make sure you have plenty of room! It is an easy game to understand so probably only needs explaining the first time you play it.

Aim: The idea of this game is to listen carefully and then move as fast as you can to secure a 'safe' place in the group circle!

YOU WILL NEED

- Nothing

HOW TO DO IT

Ask the group to form a wide circle, making sure that the young people are not standing too close together. Explain that the places where they stand in the circle are now 'safe' spots. Stand in the middle yourself so that there is effectively one place too little to accommodate the whole group in the circle.

Now, walk around the outside of the circle tapping each member on the shoulder. As you touch the young person say either 'Duck', or 'Goose'. Duck means that the young person can stay where they are. Goose means that both people must run in opposite directions around the outside of the circle back to the empty 'safe' spot.

The first person back stays in the circle, the other takes a turn at walking around the outside of the circle to select the next Goose.

The game ends when everyone has had a go at both roles.

11 APPLE PIE

This game works best with young people you have already met a few times as it relies on trust! It is a good warm-up to sessions around honesty and friendship.

Aim: The activity is a guessing game, but only works if the group trust the facilitator and each other enough to follow the rules.

YOU WILL NEED

- Nothing

HOW TO DO IT

Ask the group to form a wide circle and sit down. Make sure that the young people are not sitting too close together or the game won't work properly.

Explain that this activity is a guessing game to see how well the group knows each other and how good they are at disguising themselves!

Ask each young person to close their eyes tightly and not to open them unless they feel a light tap on their shoulder. Stress the importance of this request and explain that the game will not work effectively if anyone cheats. The only person with their eyes open in this game should be the person whose turn it is to 'tap'!

When a participant is tapped they should stand up and walk around the outside of the circle, selecting someone else to tap. As they do this they say 'Apple pie' quietly, trying to disguise their own voice as much as possible to confuse their friend.

The person who has been touched can then make a guess, still with their eyes closed, as to who tapped them. If they are right it is their turn to choose, if not the first person selects again until someone recognises them!

12 CLAPPING GAME

This introduction to a session works best with groups of children and young people who do not know each other well. Once again, you can make it harder by speeding up the pace as you go around the group.

Aim: The aim of the game is to go around the circle introducing the group to each other and the youth workers.

YOU WILL NEED

- Nothing!

HOW TO DO IT

Ask the young people to make a large circle, standing about arms length apart and then sit down.

Start off the game yourself by clapping twice and saying your name. Each young person then does the same. Place your co-worker somewhere in the second half of the circle so that they can help maintain the rhythm.

Once the circle is completed, start again. This time slapping twice on your knees, clap hands twice and motion to yourself, say your name and then motion to the person on your left and introduce them.

Continue around the group so that everyone introduces themselves and someone else.

If anyone makes a mistake they are 'out' and should put their legs out in front of them into the circle. The group carries on until only the person who remembers the most names is left.

You can repeat this again at the next group meeting to see how many names have been remembered!

13 FRUIT SALAD!

This icebreaker works best with groups of eight or more, with both young people and youth workers taking part. If you have a smaller group use less fruit!

Aim: The game encourages participation and listening skills. It is a good warm-up to use with a new group.

YOU WILL NEED

- Nothing

HOW TO DO IT

Ask the young people to each take a chair and form a big circle. The chair marks a 'home' place. A youth worker begins the game by standing in the middle of the circle and labelling each participant as an 'apple, orange, lemon or pear'. This should include the youth workers!

The youth worker in the middle then calls out the name of one of the fruits, for example, apples. All apples then swap places, running as fast as they can to another chair, including the youth worker. Make sure the group is clear that they cannot just stand up and sit back down on their own seat!

The person left without a home chair goes into the middle and calls another fruit and attempts to regain a chair. At any time the person in the middle can call 'Fruit salad!' and everyone has to move.

Make sure that the group is well spaced out or there could be an accident with chairs skidding into each other!

The game ends when everyone has had a go in the middle or is too out of breath to continue!

14 A NAME GAME

This is a good icebreaker for young people of any age. You can set themes or restrictions to make the game as easy or as hard as you like!

Aim: To start a session by introducing the group to each other and the youth workers.

YOU WILL NEED

- Nothing!

HOW TO DO IT

Ask the young people to form a circle facing each other. Explain that what you want is for each person to say their name and use an adjective to describe themselves. There is a catch! It has to be positive and it has to be a word that begins with the same letter as their name. Finally, no-one can duplicate the adjectives no matter how many people there are in the group with the same name!

If you think the group will be shy about this, start the process off yourself and encourage the young people to be as creative as they can. This is usually a fairly easy activity ... unless your name is Zoey and she assures me that the only adjective you can use is zany!

You can vary this by asking the group to introduce their name and an animal they like that starts with the same letter. For example, 'My name is Henry and I like hedgehogs' or 'My name is Zoey and I like zebras'.

Go around the circle until everybody has introduced himself or herself.

15 WORD TENNIS

This is a word skills game that encourages young people to use their vocabulary and think fast. If you know that your group will find the task tricky, slow the game down and take out the penalty clause.

Aim: To listen to what each player is saying and think of an appropriate response.

YOU WILL NEED

- Nothing

HOW TO DO IT

Choose two young people to start the game off. If you think that they will be reluctant to begin with, choose one person and play yourself to demonstrate the idea.

Ask someone else in the group to select a category to play 'tennis' with. Encourage them to choose something that everyone is likely to know a bit about, for example, vegetables or countries of the world, rather than anything too specialist such as ice hockey players' names.

The two young people then take it in turns to play word tennis by offering examples of the category to each other as fast as they can.

If they make a mistake and say something that is not part of the selected group then they are 'out' and a new challenger is chosen to take on the champion.

You can introduce a time penalty clause so if there is a gap of ten seconds between players' answers, they are 'out'. This makes sure that no-one deliberates for ages and takes all the turns. Keep going until one opponent cannot think of anything else to say. A new member of the group then steps forward to take up the challenge and a new category suggested.

If you have a smaller group keep going until you have one champion. If the group is large, stop when everyone has either played word tennis or elected a category for players.

16 FOLLOW MY LEADER

This is a fun warm-up game that encourages children and young people to mime. As the emphasis is on showing clearly to others what you are doing it is a good icebreaker for sessions in the Expressing Yourself section.

Aim: To introduce mime and drama activities to the group.

YOU WILL NEED

- A set of FOLLOW MY LEADER cards

HOW TO DO IT

Select a member of the group to start the game and hand them a card from the FOLLOW MY LEADER pile. Stress that they need to keep whatever is on it a secret from the rest of the group. If you know reading may be an issue for the group, set the game up so that the young person takes a card and leaves the room with you. You can then read it to them so that no-one feels worried or anxious about the task.

The person with the card then mimes whatever is on it. The rest of the group watch and raise a hand if they think they can guess what is being done. If the young person guesses the mime correctly it is their go to take a card and start the process again.

The game ends when everyone has had the opportunity to mime a card.

FOLLOW MY LEADER

Reading a book	Waking up	Singing
Playing basketball	Hammering a nail in	Catching a ball
Washing dishes	Digging a hole	Eating spaghetti
Parking a car	Having a wash	Putting on make-up
Jumping on a trampoline	Surfing	Counting money
Riding a motorbike	Playing netball	Picking flowers
Watching tennis	Eating an ice-cream	Ironing clothes
Combing your hair	Walking upstairs	Brushing your teeth
Eating chips	Hanging out washing	Fishing
Washing the car	Listening to a Walkman	Walking a dog

17 HANDSHAKE

This is a basic method of introducing the group to each other in a non-threatening way.

Aim: The aim is for young people to get to know each other's names and the youth workers when the group first comes together.

YOU WILL NEED

- Nothing

HOW TO DO IT

Set a group task for all the young people to meet every member of the group within a given time limit. This will depend on the size of the group and the ages of the young people.

Explain that the process for this is going to be to shake hands with the nearest member of the group, say your name and something that you enjoy doing then listen as the other person does the same. Highlight the importance of listening to what is being said. For example: 'Hello, I'm Claire and I like reading Harry Potter books.' 'Hello Claire, I'm Jake and I like skateboarding.'

Stress that you do not expect anyone to remember everyone's name after this initial warm-up, but that this is an opportunity to speak to the whole group.

At the end of the time limit stop the young people and ask the group to come together. Encourage the young people to introduce someone that they have just met to the rest of the group.

18 BALL GAME

This is a faster version of the previous game, which can be a great way of everyone in the group getting to know each other. Be aware of the group dynamics and make sure that the ball is being thrown to and not at anyone!

Aim: To share information within the group and to enable young people and workers to get to know each other's name.

YOU WILL NEED

- A small, soft ball

HOW TO DO IT

Gather the group together. You could form a circle but it is not essential. However, you do all need to be able to see each other.

Start the game by throwing the ball to the nearest young person giving your name and something about yourself. For example, a worker could start by saying: 'I'm Joe and I had curry for dinner!' or 'My name is Fiona and my dog is a Great Dane'. It is best to choose something that is memorable or funny, but not confrontational like football teams. This will depend on the group.

As the ball is caught the person holding it repeats what has been said and then introduces themselves. For example: 'His name is Joe and he had curry for dinner. My name is Sam and I had chips!' The smaller the group the further apart they need to stand to make this work effectively. Try and ensure that the ball is thrown to everyone and that the entire group has taken part.

If the task becomes too easy for the young people, the game can be made harder by asking the young people to stand on one leg or catch the ball with only one hand!

The game ends when everybody has been introduced to each other.

19 I WENT TO THE NORTH POLE...

This is one of those silly games that always seems to go down well! I have used it with a wide age range – older young people join in even if they seem reluctant at first! The larger the group the harder the task.

Aim: The game uses body language and encourages the young people to be observant and to look as well as listen to what is being said.

YOU WILL NEED

- Nothing

HOW TO DO IT

Before the young people arrive set up a large circle of chairs.

Once everyone is seated and can easily see each other either you or another youth worker begins the game by saying 'I went to the North Pole and I bought... a loaf of bread, or a football, or a tiger, or a bunch of flowers'. It can be absolutely anything, but while saying it you either cross your legs or fold your arms.

The game is about not only listening to what is said but also watching who says it. As you go around the circle the rest of the group have to respond 'yes you did' or 'no you didn't' depending if the right body language is copied. Make sure you seat your co-worker somewhere in the middle of the group so that if no-one has got the idea yet they can demonstrate again.

Once the young people begin to catch on to what they should be doing to get a 'yes' answer they must not tell those who have not yet worked out the pattern.

Keep going around the circle building up a huge and usually increasingly ridiculous list of things collected from the North Pole until everyone has sussed it out!

20 PAPER TOWERS

This initial team-building activity is used to encourage young people to plan and work together. Any size group can take part as you can split into teams.

Aim: For the young people to work together to achieve a shared goal.

YOU WILL NEED

- Newspaper
- Sticky tape
- A watch

HOW TO DO IT

Divide the young people into teams with no more than six in each group. Explain that the task is to plan and then construct paper towers. The object is to build the highest tower without it collapsing. You can set a penalty with older groups so that the team is disqualified if the tower falls down before the winners are announced.

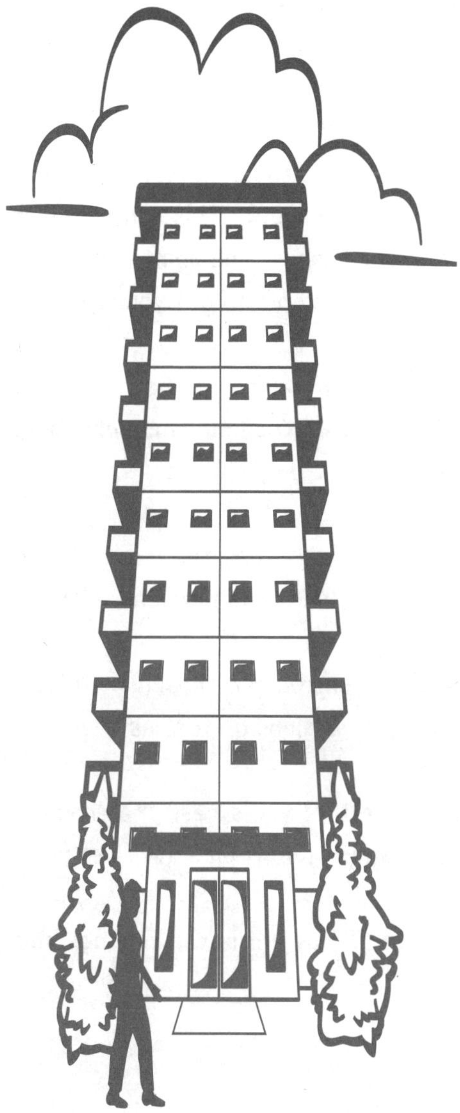

Hand out newspaper and sticky tape. Remind the group during the planning stages that this construction should be a team effort so each member of the group should contribute. No building should take place without the whole group's approval.

Give the groups 15 minutes to build their towers – and stand well back!

Call time up and invite the young people to look at each team's tower. Declare a winner and then demolish!!!

21 BELGIUM RACES

This is called Belgium races because it was shown to us on a Belgium exchange residential. It is another game that works well with larger groups, needs a lot of space and is best played at full volume!

Aim: This is a team-building warm-up exercise, which offers the children an opportunity to interact with each other and the youth workers.

YOU WILL NEED

- A beanbag

HOW TO DO IT

Ask the young people to form a large circle and stand facing each other. Choose a song that everyone knows. This can be anything from songs sung at school to Christmas carols to *Westlife* songs. The point is that everybody should be able to join in. If you think that you will not be able to get your group to sing you could use a tape or CD.

Select a volunteer to be the first 'leader', ask them to leave the circle and hand them the beanbag. As everyone in the circle begins to sing, the leader walks around the outside as many times as they choose.

When they feel ready the leader stops between two members of the circle and holds the beanbag in their palm between them.

The two young people chosen then leave the circle and run around the circumference in opposite directions as fast as they can to try and 'claim' the beanbag.

Make sure that you stress the ground rules that the person holding the beanbag cannot tussle to maintain it and the first person to reach it is the next leader.

Continue to play until everyone has had the opportunity to race for the beanbag.

22 WINK MURDER

If you have a really large group you could have more than one 'wink murderer' at a time in the group to make it harder and add to the suspense!

Aim: The aim of this icebreaker is to solve the mystery, and offers young people the opportunity to both participate and facilitate.

YOU WILL NEED

- Nothing

HOW TO DO IT

The group sits on the floor in a circle where they can see each other but are not too close. The facilitator asks them to shut their eyes. While the group can't see, the facilitator walks around the outside of the circle and taps a group member on the shoulder. They then become the wink murderer for this game.

The wink murderer has to discreetly wink at other group members, who when winked at must act out various horrible deaths. They are then out for the rest of the round. Encourage the young people to really show off their ability to over-act here!

If at any time the members of the group that are still alive think they know who the killer is they must raise their hand so the facilitator can stop play. They can then say who they think the murderer is and why. If they are wrong they have to die in a dramatic way too.

The person who guesses correctly then starts the process off again, selects the wink murderer and facilitates the next game.

You can play as many rounds of this as the young people want.

23 RHYTHM LEADER

This game is similar to wink murder in that it is a guessing game. It encourages children and young people to carefully watch each other and learn.

Aim: To identify who is setting the rhythm pattern within the group by closely observing body language and eye contact.

YOU WILL NEED

- Nothing

HOW TO DO IT

Seat the group in a large circle facing each other. Walk around the outside of the circle and tap one group member on the shoulder. Lead the young person that you have selected to a place where they cannot see the other participants.

Walk around the outside of the circle again and tap another person on the shoulder. They become the rhythm leader for this round.

The rhythm leader starts to clap, click their fingers or slap the floor to make a rhythm that the rest of the circle tries to follow. Invite the young person outside of the circle to re-join the group and sit down.

The rhythm leader changes tempo as and how they choose. Everyone else should copy, trying hard not to make it obvious who they are following.

At any point in the round the young person can guess who the rhythm leader is. If they are correct the rhythm leader leaves the circle to become the next person to guess.

The person who guessed correctly selects the next rhythm leader by walking around the circle and tapping a participant on the shoulder.

Repeat the process until everyone has had the opportunity to be the rhythm leader or the 'guesser'.

24 THE KEY GAME

This is a fun warm-up activity for larger groups. It works best with at least six young people.

Aim: The idea of this game is to snatch the keys from the young person guarding them without being seen!

YOU WILL NEED

- A bunch of keys
- Plenty of clear space to move about in

HOW TO DO IT

Identify one young person in the group to be the first 'guard'. If the group has already met you may want to offer this to someone who has worked hard in previous sessions or who has supported other members of the group before.

The guard stands facing the wall with the bunch of keys at their feet. Make sure they stand close to the wall but not so close that they are going to whack their head as they look up!

The rest of the group needs to stand against the opposite wall of the room facing forwards.

Explain that the object of the game is to sneak up on the young person guarding the keys and take them without the guard seeing. You can play it so that they have to crawl across the floor to reach the keys if you want to make it harder!

The main group then slowly edges towards the opposite wall as quietly as they can. The young person with the key is allowed to look round whenever they hear a sound.

If the guard sees anybody moving when they glance back, the young person who moved is disqualified and has to go back to the start.

The first person to get to the keys takes the next turn at being the guard.

25 FREEZE TAG

This is a variation on traditional 'tag' and can be a very noisy game! Make sure that the young people have enough clear space to run around.

Aim: This is a game that encourages mutual support and is a good introduction to group work. The idea is to keep as many of the group running about and to rescue anybody who has been 'frozen'.

YOU WILL NEED

- Nothing

HOW TO DO IT

Ask for a volunteer to be the first 'freeze tag'. Explain that their role is to catch other members of the group, and freeze tag them by touching them and yelling 'freeze!'

Explain to the rest of the group that they can run around trying their hardest to avoid capture by the freeze tag. If they are tagged they must freeze and stay still until set free by another young person.

To un-tag someone, other members of the group can touch the frozen young person and shout 'un-freeze'.

Once free, the young person can continue to run about and the game continues.

You should make sure that everybody has an opportunity to play both parts of the game.

26 BIRTHDAYS

You can use this warm-up game with any age and ability, but you really need more than 12 in the group for it to work well.

Aim: To enable the young people to make contact with each other and discover things they have in common.

YOU WILL NEED

- Nothing!

HOW TO DO IT

Ask the young people to move around the group and find someone born in the same month as them. If this is no challenge as they all know each other very well, choose another date that they are all likely to know, for example, a parent's birthday.

When they have found a partner, ask them to join with another pair born in the same month and repeat until the whole group is divided into months.

Once everyone is in a month group, ask the young people to share the date of their birthday and arrange themselves in descending order.

Finally, facilitate the whole group to get into a circle or line that starts with January and goes through to December. Review the process with the group.

GETTING TO KNOW EACH OTHER

27 MY TIMELINE

The idea of this exercise is to enable the child you are working with to map the important things that have happened to them in their life so far, and so explore major events that have occurred.

Aim: This process enables children and young people to discuss things that have happened to them in a safe environment. They ultimately choose how much they want to share.

YOU WILL NEED

- Flipchart paper taped together to make a timeline for the wall
- Marker pens

HOW TO DO IT

Before the young person arrives prepare the timeline by taping flipchart sheets end-to-end together along a large stretch of wall. Make sure this is set at a height that can be reached comfortably.

With a thick black marker write the words 'BIRTH' at the start of your timeline and 'NOW' at the end. Draw a straight line between the two poles half way down the paper.

Explain what the aim of the timeline is and what you are trying to produce together. Point out the straight black line between the two points. Ask the young person to consider if their life has been a straight line, i.e. nothing happening and feelings and events staying the same, or if it has been a series of high points and low that move either side of the line.

Invite the young person to take a pen and write important landmarks in the appropriate place on the timeline. This should include any event or change that has had an impact on how they feel or live, and can be placed above or below the black line as they choose. For example, when they started school, the birth of a brother or sister, parents divorcing or the death of a pet. Encourage the child to include religious celebrations and important events within their culture.

Once the timeline is complete encourage the young person to stand back and look at what has been produced. Discuss the highs and lows and how they impact on the present, including how issues could be resolved.

28 MY DESERT ISLAND

You can use this method of 'mapping' with young people of any age or gender and it works just as well in a group or individually. As it uses pictures it is an ideal tool to use with young people who find writing difficult.

Aim: To begin to understand the important people in the life of the young person.

YOU WILL NEED

- Flipchart paper
- Markers pens
- Stickers, glitter, string, etc (optional)

HOW TO DO IT

Explain to the group that you are giving them a once in a lifetime opportunity to create their own personal desert island! Go on to say that they can take anyone they like to the island, including friends, family and even pets!

Hand out the paper and art equipment. Make sure you point out that this not a drawing class, it does not matter if they use pictures, words or a mixture of both.

Allow about 15 minutes for the group to make their selections, draw their island and start to place people where they want them. Be sensitive to who is represented on the island and how young people approach the task.

Next ask them to show themselves where they would like to be.

Finally, tell them they can put anyone they don't want on their island into the sea! You can enlarge upon this by introducing sharks into the water or boats to bring those they like to see occasionally to visit the island.

Once everyone has finished ask the group if they would like to share their island with the other young people. If there is reluctance to share in the large group you could do this part in pairs. Are there similar choices for who is chosen? Who stays and who is in the sea? Who do they want to be with?

29 SPIDERS WEB MAP

This is a version of the desert island that we developed for use with young people aged 10+, who may be reluctant to create an island. It uses the same idea - the closer the person is in the web to the spider the more they like and trust them. Those at the outskirts of the web are people that they are less happy with.

Aim: To produce a map that shows the young person's family and friends and the relationships they have with them.

YOU WILL NEED

- A large sheet of paper
- Coloured felt pens

HOW TO DO IT

Explain to the young person the purpose of the spiders web map activity.

Suggest that they are the spider and ask them to choose a coloured pen to represent themselves and draw a spider in the middle of the paper. Stress that this is not a drawing class, so it does not matter how the spider is drawn - it could just be a coloured dot!

Now, using a different colour ask the child to draw lines of web to the people who are important to them. Explain that people who they are close to, for example, a parent or best friend, should be shown close to the spider. People who they are not so keen on can be shown at the end of longer web lines.

Allow about 10 minutes, dependent on the age of the child, to think through the process and map everyone.

Once they have finished, use the map as a starting base for a discussion, particularly looking at the choices they have made.

30 SHARE/NOT SHARE

This session can be adapted to work on specific issues for one-to-one work. You can change the share/not share cards to make the game age appropriate for the group you are working with.

Aim: This introduces the idea that there are parts of ourselves that we share with different people and bits that we choose to withhold. The aim is for the cards to promote discussion about what is appropriate to share, how we select and how this differs depending on our own comfort zones.

YOU WILL NEED

- 3 x pieces of card headed 'SHARE WITH FAMILY', 'SHARE WITH FRIENDS' and 'KEEP TO SELF'
- A copy of the SHARE/NOT SHARE cards

HOW TO DO IT

Explain to the young person that this is basically a sorting game. There is no wrong or right answer because it is up to them and how they feel about sharing personal information. Suggest that it may be that information is shared at different points in relationships, for example, you may choose to share things with a friend that you have known for years but not with a new member of your class.

Place the three headings in front of the group in a line from left to right. Then hand out the SHARE/NOT SHARE cards.

Once the young person is clear about what is being asked of them make the proviso that if they are unsure as to which heading a card should go under, they can pass and return to the card when they have had time to think or discuss it with you.

You can facilitate this process by questioning or challenging decisions and asking the child to explain their decision. The game ends when all the cards are sorted.

SHARE/NOT SHARE

1 I want to see my real dad

2 I hate meeting new people

3 I am worried that my body is changing

4 My mum hits me

5 I am scared to go to school

6 I am frightened of the dark

7 I think I am ugly

8 I wish I was taller

9 I wish I was thinner

10 My mum drinks too much alcohol

11 I don't know about sex and my friends do

12 I can't read very well

13 When I go to town I often shoplift

14 I have been chosen for the hockey team

15 Sometimes I make myself sick after I've eaten

16 I want to be good at maths

17 I'm not always allowed to go out

18 I have headlice

19 I don't want to live at home anymore

20 I told my sister a lie

21 I borrowed something and lost it

22 I am not sure what a French kiss is

23 I have inherited £5,000

24 I often feel that I can't cope

31 SECRETS

The aim of this activity is to encourage young people to consider the difference between 'good' secrets and 'bad' secrets. It is most effective during individual work with a young person that you already know something about. Be sensitive to what may arise from the session – you are asking the child to share their thoughts with you. Ensure that the young person is clear about your boundaries around confidentiality and that you are clear what procedures and guidelines you need to follow should they disclose.

YOU WILL NEED

- 2 x pieces of paper marked 'GOOD SECRET' and 'BAD SECRET'
- Post-it notes with 'secrets' on
- Pen
- Spare post-it notes

HOW TO DO IT

Before the young person arrives set up the room or wall you plan to use so that one side becomes the 'good secret' area and the other the 'bad secret' zone.

Introduce the session to the child by talking about secrets. Make sure that you are clear what their understanding of a secret is. Then, introduce the idea of different kinds of secrets. Are they aware of any differences?

Now explain that you are going to play a sorting game. Show the young person the post-it notes and show them that there is a different secret on each. Some are gender specific so you will need to change them as appropriate. Hand the pile over and ask the child to stick the secrets in different zones. If they are unsure of where one should go invite them to stick it somewhere in the middle.

Keep a dialogue going throughout the process asking the child to explain their decision and talk around any issues raised. Once they have completed the task review what has happened together.

You may want to invite the child to write their own examples on the spare notes and stick them in the appropriate areas. Record any concerns or issues that need to be raised at the next session.

SECRETS

1 Your brother smashed a window at home and has told you not to tell anyone

2 Your friend has stolen money from school – she says she will go halves with you if you don't tell

3 It is your mate's birthday and her mum is going to throw a surprise party

4 You have caught your little sister smoking – she begs you not to tell your dad

5 School sent home a letter marked 'Urgent – for attention of parent only' – you opened it, do you tell anyone?

6 Your friend went shoplifting and gave you loads of stuff to hide

7 Your friend said she was playing round at your house last night – but she went down the town

8 Your sister tells you she is really worried – she thinks she may be pregnant

9 Someone is trying to make you do something you don't want to

10 You haven't done your homework so you tell your teacher you have lost your book

11 A boy from school phones but you don't want to speak to him – you get your sister to say you are out.

12 You have hidden all your family's Christmas presents under your bed

13 You tell your mum you came top in a maths test – you didn't

14 Your mum locks you in your room if you behave badly – she tells you not to tell your dad

15 You see your dad kiss another woman at Christmas – he insists you don't tell anyone

16 You want to send a Valentine's card to someone at school

17 You are spending your dinner money on chocolate and crisps – your mum thinks you are eating lunch

18 You arrive home late and tell your dad that the bus was cancelled

19 You have a secret diary that you write all your thoughts in

20 At youth club someone breaks into the tuck shop and steals the sweets. You are offered cheap chocolate at school

21 You and your sister plan a treat for your mum for Mother's Day

22 The phone bill arrives and it is really high – you tell everyone that it was not you

32 THE TRUTH, THE WHOLE TRUTH...

This worksheet explores the sensitive issue of telling the truth and honesty. It works best in one-to-one settings because the young people can be more open about their feelings without any peer pressure.

Aim: To provoke discussion around the consequences of telling the truth or choosing to lie.

YOU WILL NEED

- A copy of the worksheet
- Pens

HOW TO DO IT

Start the session with a brief discussion about the difference between telling the truth and lying. Make sure that you are clear about the child's understanding and be prepared to explore issues raised, for example, adults not telling the truth to the child in the past.

Hand out a copy of the worksheet and a pen. Consider the young person's literacy abilities and decide if you are going to support them by reading out each statement or leaving them to do this alone.

Once the young person has decided which box to tick, look through the worksheet together.

Explore the consequences of each statement, for example, if they have ticked 'that's me' next to one of the statements about withholding information ask them to consider what the positive and negative outcomes of that action might be. Similarly encourage empathy for other people's feelings in the examples given. How does their parent/carer feel if they don't come home on time and lie about where they have been? How do they feel if someone lies to them?

Close the session by thinking of three examples where it is vital to tell the truth.

THE TRUTH, THE WHOLE TRUTH...

Look at the statements below and consider how true they are for you. Please put a tick in the box that is most like you.

	That's me	That's sometimes me	That's not me
Sometimes I tell a lie to get out of trouble			
I don't always tell my parent/carer where I have been			
At school I say I am ill to get out of lessons			
I know it is important to tell the truth			
If a police officer asked me questions, I would tell her/him the truth			
I sometimes lie about my age to get into the cinema			
If a teacher asked about my friend I wouldn't tell on him/her			
I often tell people I have got things that I haven't			
If my sister asks if I like her new clothes I say 'yes' even if I don't			
Sometimes I pretend I can't hear my mum when she tells me to do something			
If I found £20 at school I would pretend it was mine			

33 THIS IS ME!

This is a fun way of encouraging young people to share things about themselves and to get an idea of what motivates them. This works just as well as a group or individual activity.

Aim: To produce a collage plate that represents the young person's personality.

YOU WILL NEED

- Large paper plates
- Glue
- Scissors
- Marker pens
- Newspapers
- Magazines
- Varnish

HOW TO DO IT

Make sure you have a good range of age appropriate magazines and pictures.

Suggest that the young people work in groups of four and hand out scissors, glue, magazines and paper plates. If you are doing this as part of a one-to-one session share this process with the child, discussing their choices as you go along.

Explain to the group that the idea is for each person to produce a plate that represents their personality. This can include the good and bad bits! Offer a few examples – their favourite pop star, or pictures that show how they may be feeling today. If the young people look a bit unsure you and your co-worker could have a go at making one too.

Encourage the children to 'own' their plates by signing the collage with a decorative version of their name. The glitter glue is really effective for this!

Once everyone has finished invite the young people to display their plates, sharing the bits they feel comfortable with the group.

Finally, when the glue has dried varnish the plates to seal the pictures and use them to decorate the group area.

34 ATTITUDE SCALE

This is a good way to start work around self-esteem and encouraging young people to say what they want. It introduces the idea of assertive and passive behaviour.

Aim: To encourage the young people to think about how they see themselves and consider how this compares with how others perceive them.

YOU WILL NEED

- Nothing

HOW TO DO IT

Explain to the young people that the aim of this activity is to develop an attitude scale, to show the personalities within the group ranging from assertive to passive. You may need to offer further explanation of what you mean by assertive and passive. The scale should form a straight line and include everyone.

Decide which end of your scale is assertive and which end is passive and make sure that the young people are clear about this.

Allow five to ten minutes (depending on the size of the group) for the young people to decide where they think they should stand on the scale. Position yourself on the scale too.

When everybody is comfortable with his or her position on the scale, stop.

Ask the young people to look around them and reflect on what they see. Are there any surprises? Does how they see themselves fit in with other people's perceptions of them? What about the youth workers? Discuss the positive and negative points of both ends of the scale.

35 COLOURS

This activity encourages young people to discuss their feelings and emotions. It can be used either individually or with groups, but is most effective with small groups.

Aim: To look at colours and the feelings associated with them.

YOU WILL NEED

- Pens
- Squares of card in assorted colours

HOW TO DO IT

Begin the session by introducing the idea that colours can represent feelings and emotions. Make sure that you stress that this is not an exact science! Different colours may mean different things to different people. A good example of this is the colour red - anger or passion?

Once the group has grasped the idea ask them to work individually or in pairs.

Hand out a good selection of coloured squares with a pen to each pair. Ask the young people to look carefully at the squares and think about what feelings or emotions they associate with the colours. Then, use a pen to write the word on the colour. If a colour evokes a different response from each partner, write both words on the card.

When everybody has finished ask the whole group to form a circle and discuss their findings. Is there any pattern or theme emerging? Are there many cards with two or more words on? What colours would the group choose to decorate a room to relax in? To have a party in? To do homework in?

Finally ask each young person to choose a colour to represent how they feel now to close the session.

36 HELPING HAND

This session can be done either as a group or one-to-one activity. It is a good start to a project looking at keeping safe and protective behaviour.

Aim: To encourage the young people to identify people they could talk to if they were worried or concerned about an issue.

YOU WILL NEED

- Paper
- Pens

HOW TO DO IT

Before you start consider the make up of your group and how much you know about them. If you have not worked with the group before you will need to be careful to keep the information discussed depersonalised by referring only to the examples below. If you know the group well you can ask them to think of their own situations. Be careful that you do not encourage the young people to make disclosures unless you have the appropriate support in place.

Ask the group to form a circle or to sit so that they can all hear you and contribute. Choose one of the situations below and read it out to the young people.

'John is 10, wears glasses and is the smallest in his class. He hates sports, but is really good at maths and always comes top in tests. The other kids all laugh and call him "boffin" and "goody-goody" and "teacher's pet" and take his glasses out of his bag and throw them to each other in the cloakroom...'

'Cherish is 9 and friends with some older girls who live on the same estate. The older girls have just started stealing things from the local shop. Cherish has not taken anything, but she has eaten some stolen sweets the girls gave her. Now the others in the group are saying that they won't let her hang around with them if she does not steal too...'

Then ask the question: 'How do you think John/Cherish feels?' and facilitate a discussion around the answers given.

Now ask the group to start to imagine that they are in a similar situation. Explain that they do not have to share what they are thinking, but suggest that they start to identify people that they could tell and ask for help.

Hand out the paper and pens and ask each young person to draw around one of their hands in the centre of their sheet.

Now explain that the thumb on the hand represents the first person that they would go to if they were in trouble and needed help. Ask them to write down whom they would go to next if the first person wasn't in or would not listen. Carry on until all five fingers have names.

Reflect on the process with the group. Was it easy to identify a support network? Will it change often? What is it about these people that makes them special and different to others they know?

37 WOULD YOU EVER?

This sheet is best used with small groups of children or young people that you feel are at risk of becoming involved in offending behaviour. You will need to have a good relationship with them so that they feel they can be honest.

The young people's responses will define any follow-up sessions. These should highlight the choices that can be made and the consequences of getting involved with behaviour that is likely to lead to offending.

Aim: To identify offending behaviour within the group. To assess the need for preventative work and the issues and concerns for the young people.

YOU WILL NEED

- Some information about the impact that the 1998 Crime and Disorder Act has on children over 10 in an age appropriate form
- Copies of the sheet
- Pens

HOW TO DO IT

When you first introduce this activity you will need to re-assure the young people that what they share will remain confidential, unless it is a child protection issue or you are required to pass it on to the police. You will have to assess the group and their level of offending to see if this is going to be a major issue.

Also, make sure that the group realises that you are not suggesting that you think they have done any or all of the entire list!

If you know that the group has a short attention span cut the number of questions you ask. Similarly you could read the questions out.

Pick out any issues that you want the group to explore and facilitate a discussion. Provide information and ask if the group would like to focus on one or two issues to work on over the next few weeks.

If you want to use this as part of your project evaluation, ask the questions once at the start of your involvement and again towards the end to see if there is any change in attitudes or behaviour. You will need to code the sheets so you know who said what!

WOULD YOU EVER?

For every question please answer yes or no.

	Yes	No
Text abuse to someone you don't like		
Call someone names in the street		
Give a false name to the police		
Steal something from a shop		
Steal money from your friends		
Steal money from home		
Steal things from home to sell		
Be unkind to an animal		
Throw stones at the window of a neighbour you didn't like		
Write things about another child on walls		
Damage cars parked in the street		
Keep money you found in the street		
Hit someone who called you names		
Use someone else's mobile phone without asking		
Travel on a bus or train without paying		

38 FEELINGS FILE

This encourages children to focus on a specific feeling and recall the events surrounding it. It is a good prelude to activities in the next section that look at how emotions are expressed.

Aim: For young people to begin to associate feelings with events and actions.

YOU WILL NEED

- Copies of the 'FEELINGS FILE' sheet
- Pens

HOW TO DO IT

Ask the young people to choose a partner each. If there is an uneven number in the group work in threes. Hand out pens and a copy of the FEELINGS FILE sheet to each member of the group.

Explain that during this exercise individuals are free to choose how much they want to share and have the right to withhold things they do not want to discuss. This gives everyone the opportunity to only choose examples that they feel comfortable with.

Ask the young people to read the sheet on their own, looking at each feeling and thinking about a time when they felt like this. For example, a time when they felt angry may be last night during an argument with their brother over what to watch on television.

When everyone has had time to think about the task and select words that reflect their experience, ask him or her to share their sheet with their partner.

Spend time comparing and discussing what has been written. Are they similar? Expand upon what situations these feelings might be associated with. Ask the young people to discuss how they handle different situations, for example, feeling lonely or excited.

Close the session by asking the group to each choose a word to describe how they feel now.

FEELINGS FILE

A time that I felt happy was when ....

A time that I felt angry was when ....

A time that I was excited was ....

I last felt sad when ....

The last time I was lonely was ....

A time that I felt loved was when ....

A person who makes me feel listened to is ....

A person who makes me laugh is ....

A person who makes me feel loved is ....

A person whom I trust is ....

Someone who makes me feel bad about myself is ....

Someone who does not help me is ....

Someone that I can talk to about these things is ....

39 THINGS ABOUT ME

This is a good way to initiate conversation during a first session. You can use the worksheet with any age from 9+, but it is not appropriate for a group activity.

Aim: To encourage the child to focus on positive aspects of themselves and identify areas that they would like support with.

YOU WILL NEED

- Coloured pens
- A copy of the 'THINGS ABOUT ME – SIGNPOST' sheet

HOW TO DO IT

Before you hand out the signpost sheet to the child you are working with spend some time talking about the aim of the worksheet and what you would like them to produce. Explain that the process will enable you to understand their interests, wishes and needs and that they can tell you as much or as little as they choose. Make sure that you are clear about child protection procedures and your responsibilities in the event of a disclosure.

Give the worksheet to the young person and allow them time and space to think about their responses. If the child is struggling make some suggestions to illustrate what you are asking. For example, a thing they do well may be drawing or playing football; something they would like to work on is controlling their anger.

Look at their completed signpost together. What was easiest, thinking of positive things about themselves or focusing on the areas that they are not so happy with?

Work together on an action plan to address issues raised over the next sessions planned and give a copy to the young person so that you are both clear about the aims of your meetings.

THINGS ABOUT ME - SIGNPOST

Have a look at the signpost below, and use the spaces to write key words that describe you. Think of things you do well, what is special about you and things you like and put these on the white signs. On the grey signs put things you think are not going so well or that you would like help with.

EXPRESSING YOURSELF

40 PICTURE PAIRS

This is a matching game that can be used with young people who have difficulties in reading and prefer to work with pictures. You can either facilitate the game between two players or play the game with the young person as part of an individual plan.

Aim: To encourage children to recognise non-verbal signals and expressions and so respond appropriately to situations.

YOU WILL NEED

- A set of cards
- Spare cards.

HOW TO DO IT

Before the session prepare by making up the cards. You can be as creative as you like with the pictures, but remember to make a matching pair for each one. These could be simple hand drawn images of faces expressing different feelings, for example, happy smiles or angry frowns. Another method is to cut faces out of magazines and paste them onto cards. Make sure that you have a good range of expressions.

Place the cards face down on the table and muddle them up so that the pairs are not together. Explain to the child that this is a game of memory and that they need to watch what is happening.

Take it in turns to turn over two cards and look at the pictures. Encourage the child to tell you what the person on the card is feeling and discuss how this is recognised.

If the cards are the same they form a pair and can be collected. If not, once you have identified the face, place it face down back in the same position.

The person to make up the most pairs wins.

41 ACT OUT FEELINGS!

This activity can be used as a taster for more indepth drama/role play sessions to address specific issues. It should be played at a fairly fast pace so that everybody has the chance to act out a character.

Aim: To introduce the group to role play and drama-based activities. It also enables group members to act out issues which may be relevant to them in a safe environment.

YOU WILL NEED

- A copy of the set of 'ACT OUT' cards
- Information around issues likely to be raised through the session, e.g. bullying

HOW TO DO IT

Start the session with a short discussion about how non-verbal communication often shows others how we are feeling or behaving without any words being spoken. Ask the young people to consider how true this is and to think about their own body language.

Next, explain that you are going to ask for a volunteer to demonstrate this. Introduce the set of cards you have and the game. Tell the group that while one person is acting out what is on the card, the others should ask questions to try and guess what is on the card. All questions must be answered in character so, for example, if your card says 'feeling angry', you can reply to the question 'How are you?' by shouting, 'What has it got to do with you?'

If you are met with a shy silence, volunteer yourself or your co-worker to take the first turn. Often this is a great success, especially if you really over act!

A guess can be made at any stage in the process. If it is correct then the person who guessed takes a new card and begins again. If the guess is wrong continue until someone gets it right. Try and keep the questions moving along so that the game keeps pace.

This should be a game that is thought provoking, but is good fun. Be aware that some cards may be uncomfortable for the young person who draws it to act out. For example, a young person who has been the victim of a bully may not be happy to act out being scared or even a bully. You will need to be sensitive to the group's needs and if necessary swap cards.

ACT OUT CARDS

Feeling scared
Being a bully
Being bullied
Feeling happy
Feeling upset
Feeling proud
Feeling disappointed
Feeling lonely
Being selfish
Feeling anxious
Feeling frustrated
Feeling confident
Feeling bored
Feeling angry

42 TALK, TALK

This discussion is aimed at young people who have poor social skills and find it hard to make friends or express themselves clearly. The idea can be adapted to suit either a group or an individual and works well with the next activity.

Aim: To consider the differences between talking to and talking with someone. The discussion promotes conversation and develops verbal communication skills.

YOU WILL NEED

- Marker pens
- Two large sheets of flipchart paper

HOW TO DO IT

Before the young people arrive stick up the two sheets of paper so that the whole group can see them. Write the heading 'TALKING' on the top of one sheet and 'CONVERSATION' on the other.

Explain the aim of the session and ask for two volunteers. Make sure you facilitate this bit carefully, bearing in mind the literacy skills within the group.

Ask the group to consider what they think the differences are between talking and having a conversation.

Hand each volunteer a marker pen and ask him or her to write down suggestions from the group. If the response is slow to begin with make some suggestions. For example:

Talking
Saying things
Telling things that are important to you

Conversation
Talking and listening
Sharing information

Once the young people have exhausted their ideas facilitate a discussion around the points raised.

43 REFLECTIVE LISTENING

This introduces the concept of reflective listening to the group. It develops conversational skills and encourages interest in what others say. You can use the activity with any size group as the young people are asked to work in threes/fours.

Aim: To focus the group on a discussion which will enable them to get to know each other quickly. If the children are already friends then it should highlight things that they don't know about each other. It encourages the young people to listen carefully to what is being said and to think about it, rather than cutting in with their own opinions.

YOU WILL NEED

- Nothing

HOW TO DO IT

Depending on the numbers of children you have in the group ask them to work in threes or fours. If it is a really small group it does work in pairs. Discuss confidentiality at this stage and reach the agreement that what is shared in the group stays there. This should encourage the participants to feel safe about talking personally.

Specify a topic to discuss within the group: 'What people usually think about me when they first meet me is…' You can demonstrate this by giving an example to start them off: 'What people think about me when they first meet me is that I have a good sense of humour!'

Set a ground rule that only one member can talk at a time in the group and that the others should listen and think about what is being said.

Once each child has had their say, discuss the information given within the groups. How similar was what your friend said to what you actually thought when you first met them? Does your self-image correspond to what others think of you?

Feedback anything that the small groups wish to share with the larger group. Are there similar themes and issues?

44 DON'T LAUGH AT ME!

This worksheet can be used in a group setting, but works best in a one-to-one situation where young people have more time to think through the issues raised.

Aim: To reflect on how it feels to be laughed at and build empathy for other children who may be in that situation. It also encourages children to consider strategies for coping with bullying and to identify who could offer them support.

YOU WILL NEED

- A copy of the 'DON'T LAUGH AT ME!' sheet for each child
- Pens

HOW TO DO IT

Introduce the idea that laughter can be used to make people feel uncomfortable and stupid as well as a way of expressing how happy we are. Explain that this is the difference between laughing at someone and with them.

Hand out the worksheet and ask the child to consider how they feel if someone laughs at them. This could be a gang at school, or a parent or sibling. Encourage them to share the experience and write down how it made them feel on the sheet.

Discuss what the young person could do if this happened again, for example, walk away and tell a trusted adult or friend. Spend time doing this and then ask the young person to use the storyboard on the sheet to show what they could do in each situation.

Review what they have drawn. Is this a solution that is going to resolve the issue or cause more trouble? Ask them to consider what they would do if the person being laughed at were someone they did not like? Would their response be different?

Finally, agree 'safe' people to approach for support if this should happen to them.

DON'T LAUGH AT ME!

How does it feel when people laugh at you? ....

....

If I was being laughed at I could . . .

If someone else was being laughed at I could . . .

45 IMAGES

This activity works on the assumption that how we see ourselves and how we are seen is not always the same. You will need to be sensitive to the group dynamics and make sure no-one takes this as an opportunity to make individuals feel uncomfortable or excluded.

Aim: The idea of the activity is for young people to explore the idea that how they perceive themselves is not necessarily how others view them. It encourages discussion around public image and first impressions and questions the importance of this.

YOU WILL NEED

- 2 x copies of the IMAGES sheet for each participant (in two different colours)
- Pens

HOW TO DO IT

Explain the aim of the session to the group and ask the young people to choose a partner to work with. Hand each person two copies of the IMAGES sheet (one of each colour) and a pen.

Now ask them to turn away from their partner and have a brief look at the sheet. Working with their back to their partner ask each person to complete both sheets:

Sheet 1:
Tick all the boxes alongside words that they think describes the partner they are working with.

Sheet 2:
Tick all the boxes next to words that they think describes themselves.

Allow up to 15 minutes for everybody to complete the task, and then ask the young people to turn around and face their partner. Each partner in turn then feeds back what they have ticked and compares this with how their partner sees him or herself. Are these the same? Are characteristics seen in different ways? For example, a young person may have ticked 'is very shy' about himself or herself, but their partner sees this as 'often feels sad'. Encourage the young people to focus on positive attributes and discuss areas of difference.

IMAGES

This person ...

Has a good sense of humour	Is very confident
Listens to other people's opinions	Often tells lies
Supports friends who need it	Is good at understanding other people
Is very shy	Doesn't make friends easily
Does not blame other people if something goes wrong	Doesn't smile very often
Is honest and trustworthy	Is very aggressive
Loses their temper often	Likes telling other people's secrets
Is fun to be with	Is always boasting about things that they have
Is creative and full of ideas	Likes sport and team games
Can be moody at times	Is a popular member of the group
Shouts a lot if people don't agree	Explains things to others well
Often feels left out	Often feels sad
Tells tales on other people	Is rude to others

One way to describe this person is ....

46 LATE FOR SCHOOL!

This provides the opportunity for young people to re-write a typical scenario the way they think it should be! Depending on how big your group is you can do a storyboard for as many characters as you like that shows the different perspectives when a young person is late for school - again! If you are working individually ask the young person to create just one story line that shows all the characters.

Aim: To encourage young people to think of the consequences of oversleeping and getting to school late and the impact this has on different family members as well as themselves.

YOU WILL NEED

- A storyboard sheet for each group
- Pens

HOW TO DO IT

Read out the following scenario to the whole group

'You stayed up late last night to watch your favourite TV programme. Your mum is calling you to get up but all you want to do is turn over and go back to sleep. You know this is the second time this week you have not made it to school on time and school has already noticed. Why does your mum always make such a fuss about everything? It's only maths first lesson and everyone knows you are no good at that. Perhaps you could go in later?'

In groups of three or four using the storyboard sheet ask the young people to construct a comic strip which shows what happens next.

Give each group the task of telling the story from a different character's point of view:

- the young person;
- the mum or dad;
- the young person's friend; or
- the teacher.

Encourage the groups to think about the consequences of any actions taken, what could have been done differently, what could be done to resolve the conflict.

LATE FOR SCHOOL!

Use the storyboard to show what happens next…

47 THAT MAKES ME ANGRY!

This works best when done individually. It encourages children and young people to begin to identify anger triggers and so develop anger management techniques.

Aim: For a young person to consider the things that make them angry and discuss ways that they could cope in that situation.

YOU WILL NEED

- A copy of the THAT MAKES ME ANGRY sheet
- Pens

HOW TO DO IT

Begin the session by talking about anger as a valid emotion that everyone feels at some time. Ask the children and young people to try and remember the last time they were angry, what happened and what their response to the situation was.

Hand out copies of the THAT MAKES ME ANGRY sheet and ask the group to look at the statements on it. For each statement ask the children to put a tick in the box that is the nearest to how they would feel if the example happened to them.

If the children are very young, or you know that the group struggles with reading and writing, you can do this as a whole group process. Read the statement out and then ask the young people to raise their hands to the feeling that they associate with the scenario.

Once everyone has completed the work sheet, facilitate a whole group feedback session. Encourage the young people to explain why something – for example, being laughed at – makes them very angry, and another thing doesn't.

The young people should begin to identify triggers for their own anger and to realise that we all have different anger thresholds or tolerances. From this you can begin work on strategies to cope with anger and aggression.

THAT MAKES ME ANGRY!

Look at the following and tick the box that shows how this would make you feel.	Very angry	Angry	A bit angry	Not at all angry
Someone calls you a name in front of your friends				
You come last in games and everyone laughs at you				
Your neighbour blames you for breaking the fence – you didn't do it				
You are not allowed to stay up as late as your friends				
A teacher tells you to get out of class – you don't want to				
Your dad says loudly that you are 'thick' in front of your friends				
Someone steals your money at school				
A group you don't know starts shouting over to you in town				
Your sister accuses you of stealing money from her – it's true				
Someone spreads untrue rumours about you				
Your mum grounds you for being rude				
Someone tells on you and you get in trouble				
Your mum won't give you any money to go out				
Your team looses at football and the opposition fans are teasing you				
Your mobile is not as good as your mate's				
Your bike is stolen				
No one will listen to what you are trying to say				
You are late home, your mum is shouting and won't listen to your excuse				

48 I DON'T WANT TO!

This encourages young people to develop strategies to say 'no' effectively in difficult situations. I have used it both with small groups and individually. You can vary the exercise by changing the issue featured in the scenario; the storyboard can be used in any context.

Aim: To develop assertiveness in saying 'no' to peer pressure to do things the young people are uncomfortable with.

YOU WILL NEED

- A storyboard sheet for each group
- Pens

HOW TO DO IT

Read out the situation outlined below to the children. Hand out a copy of the storyboard to each member of the group and make a good selection of pens available. Using their storyboard, ask the young people to show what the character could say or do to resolve the situation.

'You are walking to school with two of your mates. They suddenly say that they are going to "bunk off" today and go to the town to hang around instead. You know you should go to school but you don't want to look silly in front of your friends by not going too. They turn round and set off for town, calling to you to hurry up. You know you will get into trouble if you get caught, but don't want to let your friends down – what can you do?'

Ask the group to come together and share storyboards. Use this as a basis for a discussion on peer pressure related back to the given scenario.

Encourage the young people to think about the consequences of the characters' actions. How they could say what they think assertively? What could they have done differently? How easy is it to say 'no' to friends? What could be done to resolve any potential conflict between the group in the story?

Any issues highlighted can be used to plan further sessions.

I DON'T WANT TO!

Use the storyboard to show what happens next...

49 MY HOME

Before you start this activity make sure that you are aware of the groups' living arrangements. For example, a child that has recently moved, is living with foster parents, or has recently had to cope with bereavement, may find it very difficult to discuss how they feel. This does not preclude using this process, but it may be too sensitive to do as a group.

Aim: To support the children and young people in expressing how they feel about 'home' and their roles and responsibilities within it.

YOU WILL NEED

- Nothing

HOW TO DO IT

Start the session by explaining that you would like the group to think about a statement that you are going to make. Explain that you would like those people who agree to raise their hands. Those that don't should keep their hands down. Make this statement:

'A home is just a place you sleep'

Once the group has voted, invite the young people to share their opinions. So, for example, Kara could say she agrees because 'it is the people not the place that make a home', but Jake may be clear that it is wrong because 'a home is somewhere you belong and are safe'.

Ensure that any ground rules around confidentiality and allowing people to speak are adhered to.

Facilitate a discussion that asks the children for suggestions of what they can do to contribute towards making their home the way they want it.

Finally, agree one thing each that they can do to make a difference for the next week. This could be something practical like picking up their dirty laundry or something such as not fighting with siblings. Review next time the group meets.

50 NAME THAT FEELING!

This worksheet encourages children and young people to identify how they feel in different circumstances and encourages them to consider solutions that will not lead to tension and aggression.

Aim: To support young people in defining their feelings and analyse problems and potential ways of dealing with them.

YOU WILL NEED

- A copy of the NAME THAT FEELING! sheet, folded into a concertina so that only the first scenario shows.

HOW TO DO IT

Begin the session by talking about the wide range of emotions that we all feel. Introduce the idea that sometimes these feelings either get in the way of how we deal with a situation or are not identified correctly. So the problem remains unresolved, or becomes larger and we feel less able to deal with it. Ask the children to think about a time when a problem got worse because of something they did or did not do. What feelings do they remember?

Hand out the NAME THAT FEELING! sheet, folded up so that only the first scenario can be seen.

Ask the group to read the situation to themselves and consider the questions posed at the top of the sheet. If you know this will be a difficult task for your group, read each scenario out to the children.

Facilitate a group feedback for each of the situations. Does the group see the problem in the same way? Do they agree which feelings that might arise? How easy is it to think through some ideas for solutions?

Finally, encourage the group to think about some examples of their own to share and work through together.

NAME THAT FEELING!

For each of the situations below think about the following:
What is the problem?
What is the feeling?
What can be done?

1 Your friend always has more pocket money than you do. It is not fair! Your mum is so mean, she says you should do some jobs around the house if you want more cash!

2 Your dad has left home to live with his new girlfriend. He said you could stay at weekends but now his girlfriend is saying that there is not enough room for you.

3 Someone at school is calling your brother names in the playground and threatening to break his electric wheelchair.

4 Your mate won an art competition at school. You are really fed up and think it must have been a fix. You know yours was better!

5 Your accent is different to the rest of your class. One girl keeps teasing you about this and making everyone laugh at you. When you try and answer back she just mimics you and everyone laughs more.

6 The class is kept in after school for something you did. Now everyone is telling you to own up or else ...

51 FEELING VALUED

It is important for young people's self-esteem to feel valued by the people they care about, and by themselves. A lack of this can lead to frustration and aggressive behaviour.

Aim: This worksheet is devised as an introduction to building self worth.

YOU WILL NEED

- Copies of the worksheet FEELING VALUED
- Pens

HOW TO DO IT

Start by introducing the idea of self-esteem and feeling good about yourself. Hand out the worksheet and some pens. If you know that the young person finds reading and writing difficult, read the sheet out and use pictures or write their answers down yourself.

Support the child as they think about the issues raised on the sheet. If they say they cannot think of anything to write, suggest they think about the last time that someone made them feel happy or loved. You can then ask prompt questions to try and expand and reflect on this.

Once they have completed the sheet, review what has been written with the young person. In particular ask them to reflect on what they have written in the final section. For example, the young person may write that they feel valued when 'their mum praises them' and a way to achieve this could be 'to walk away when my brother starts a fight rather than hitting him which upsets my mum'. Devise an action plan together to achieve some of these goals.

Review agreements made regularly to celebrate achievements and set new goals.

FEELING VALUED

This is me	Last time I felt valued was when .... It made me feel ....

People who make me feel good about myself are ....

because ....

I show them I am happy by ....

Things that make me feel good about myself are

1 ....

2 ....

3 ....

Things that I can do to help achieve this are

1 ....

2 ....

3 ....

MAKING FRIENDS

52 FRIENDSHIP LINE

This is a good way to look at friendships, past and present, and the importance of them to our personal 'history'.

Aim: To encourage each young person to create a friendship line which charts important people and their influences on their life.

YOU WILL NEED

- Sheets of flipchart paper
- Marker pens

HOW TO DO IT

Hand each member of the group a sheet of flipchart paper and place a good selection of markers close by.

Explain to the young people that they are going to make a friendship line to depict people whose friendship has been important to them from their earliest memories to the present. This can be done using words or pictures.

Next to each name ask the group to show why that person was/is important to them.

While explaining the task, stress that it is up to each person to choose how much they wish to put onto paper and share. Also point out that it does not matter how many or few people are recorded on the line – this is an exercise to look at friendships and what they mean, not a competition to see who knows the most people!

Once everyone has finished ask the group to come together and talk through the parts of their friendship line they feel comfortable sharing. Are there similarities? Have people kept in touch with their early friends? Are some friendships associated with different activities, for example, Scouts or the youth club?

53 WHAT MAKES A GOOD FRIEND?

This works well at the start of a session when you can encourage the young people to be open about their first thoughts before any discussions take place.

Aim: The aim of the activity is to identify the key features of a good friend and to encourage the children to consider what they can offer a potential relationship.

YOU WILL NEED

- Pens
- Copies of the WHAT MAKES A GOOD FRIEND? sheet

HOW TO DO IT

If you are planning this as part of a group session gather the children together into a circle. If you are working individually you could write the points on the worksheet onto a large sheet of flipchart paper and encourage them to illustrate the things that they record.

Explain to the group that the idea of the activity is to start to think about what goes into making a good friendship. Encourage the children to consider friendship as a two-way process that needs working at if it is to be successful. This means that they have a responsibility to make it work as well as the other person!

Hand out the worksheet and allow about 10 to 15 minutes for the children to complete it. This will depend on the size of your group. Ask that they work alone at the moment and stress that there are no definite right or wrong answers.

Once the group has had time to record their ideas, invite them to share what they have talked about in pairs.

Bring the children back together in a circle to discuss their ideas. Are there similar suggestions? Are some suggestions based on physical attributes or status within the group? For example, 'looking really good' or 'knowing everyone in town' may be seen as a good quality, but is it really the basis for a friendship?

Pull out the main themes and agree a group list. Display to refer to in future sessions around relationships.

WHAT MAKES A GOOD FRIEND?

Three things that I think make a good friend are

1 ....

2 ....

3 ....

What makes me a good friend is

1 ....

2 ....

3 ....

.... is my friend because ....

....

I am a good friend to them because ....

....

Good things we do together are

1 ....

2 ....

3 ....

54 MAGIC SPELL FOR A FRIEND

This is similar to the previous activity, but works well with under 11s. It encourages young people to think about what qualities they look for in a friend, what makes a person special and how to value friendship. It can be used with groups or individually.

Aim: To identify the key features that makes a trusting friendship.

YOU WILL NEED

- Copies of the MAGIC SPELL sheet
- Pens

HOW TO DO IT

Hand out the MAGIC SPELL sheets and a pen to each member of the group.

Explain that what you want them to do is think about who their ideal friend would be. Ask them to imagine that you hold a magic wand that will grant them their ideal friends if they can write the correct spell. You can be as creative as you like setting the scene dependent on the group.

This spell can summon up a real or imagined person but stress that you are asking them to consider personal qualities that they think are vital for a good friendship, not how someone looks or what they have.

When the children have had time to think ask them to list six things for their spell that they think are the most important. Ask that they do this individually at the moment. If you know that some members of your group are not confident with writing tasks, divide the group into pairs so that they can work with a child with good literacy skills.

Once they have completed the six, ask them to write in the space below the reason why this is a positive attribute and offer an example.

Make sure you allow everyone enough time to think about the task and then ask the group to break into pairs to share ideas. Encourage them to discuss their responses. Are there similarities? Are these realistic things to want in a friend? Are the characteristics that they value in others ones they think describe themselves?

MAGIC SPELL

Write a spell to conjure up a friend that will be special to you

1

This is important to me because

2

This is important to me because

3

This is important to me because

4

This is important to me because

5

This is important to me because

6

This is important to me because

55 BULLY COURT

Before you consider this project you need to be aware of the dynamics within the group you plan to work with. It may not be appropriate for someone who has either been a recent victim of bullying or who already dominates the group.

Aim: To explore the issues around bullying and to look at the different characters' involvement in a given scenario.

YOU WILL NEED

- A set of the BULLY COURT cards
- Leaflets and telephone numbers for local support networks for the victims of bullying.

HOW TO DO IT

This is a role play activity which divides up participants to work through the issues highlighted during the 'bully court'. There are no given solutions, as the young people will take the role play where they want to. The facilitator's job is to set the scene, make sure that no-one is feeling uncomfortable and that any issues raised are resolved.

Ask the group to form a circle and then read the following, changing the gender to suit your group:

'This bully court has come together to assess this situation and agree whether bullying has taken place or not. The court will then decide what should, if anything happen to the bully.

'It is alleged that two boys kicked another young person on the way home from school. One then ripped up schoolwork, spat and made further threats if this information was shared with teachers or parents. This is not the first time that an incident like this has happened. Money has also been stolen from the young person and food taken with the threat of violence if they argued back.

'The boys say that it is not their fault and that the other young person started all the trouble. They claim that the other young person does not like them and is trying to get them in trouble. Neither will comment on the stealing, spitting and threats of violence.'

Hand out a card with a character name on to each member of the group. Allow 10 minutes for each participant to think about the role that they are to play and how this could fit with the scene outlined by the facilitator.

In the meantime set up the room so that the circle you had becomes a semi-circle with one chair at the front for the judge, one for the accused and one for each witness or speaker. The rest of the group will form the jury and make decisions on what happens next based on discussion and consensus. The idea is that this represents a court.

The facilitator then invites each character in turn to step forward and tell their story to the bully court. In role, the young people can then discuss what has been said and decide whether this is a case of bullying or wrongful accusations.

Finally, facilitate a discussion about what should happen to bullies and how victims of bullying can keep themselves safe and be more assertive.

BULLY COURT CARDS

VICTIM *You have not told anyone what has been happening to you over the last months as you are scared of what might happen.*
ACCUSED *You are angry because you don't think it is your fault. Lots of people argue – what is all the fuss about?*
ACCUSED *You do not think that you should be here at all. Everyone always blames you – it's not fair.*
WITNESS *You have seen some things that have made you worried. You do not think that it is right that someone is being picked on.*
TEACHER *You teach all those involved and have stepped in before.*
WITNESS *You know what has happened but you are scared about what will happen to you if you say something.*
JUDGE *Your role is to listen to each person and make sure that you and the jury are clear what is being said*
PARENT *Your son has never been in trouble before and you don't believe it.*
PARENT *It is not just at school that your son is difficult. He is angry and aggressive at home too and you have had enough.*
PARENT *You have been getting more and more concerned recently. Your child does not want to go to school, go out, anything.*

JURY

JURY

JURY

JURY

JURY

JURY

JURY

JURY

JURY

JURY

JURY

JURY

56 FOLLOW THE CROWD

This exercise asks young people to consider the consequences of their actions in potential situations. You can alter the situations to fit with issues relevant to the children you are working with.

Aim: To encourage children to consider the losses and gains of giving in to peer pressure.

YOU WILL NEED

- Copies of the FOLLOW THE CROWD sheet
- Pens

HOW TO DO IT

Ask the young people to consider a time when they have 'followed the crowd' and done something that they knew was not right, but did it because friends did. Explain that they do not have to share this unless they really want to, but to think about the choices they had and what made the decision for them.

Hand out the FOLLOW THE CROWD sheet and a pen to each participant. Ask the group to look at each situation given and to think of what the plus and minus points for following the crowd would be. For example, if a group writes their names on the wall and you decide to join in, the plus might be that you become accepted as part of their gang. The minus point may be that a neighbour sees it, recognises you and your parents are told.

Encourage the group to think ahead as to what the consequences of their decisions may be.

When everyone has completed their sheet, encourage the young people to discuss potential plus and minus points for each scenario.

Conclude by facilitating a discussion that looks at ways that the young person in the situations could have been assertive and said 'no' without losing face within the peer group.

FOLLOW THE CROWD

Think about the plus and minus points about joining in with the following situations.

1 Joining in with a group that are bullying another child at school

PLUS .... MINUS ....

2 Joining in with a group that are being unkind to a stray cat

PLUS .... MINUS ....

3 Joining in with a group who are cheating in a game against younger children

PLUS .... MINUS ....

4 Joining in with a friend who is lying to his parents to get out of trouble

PLUS .... MINUS ....

5 Joining in with a group that is staying out in the street later than they are allowed

PLUS .... MINUS ....

6 Joining in with a friend who is taking other children's things without asking

PLUS .... MINUS ....

7 Joining in with a group who are being rude to a teacher

PLUS .... MINUS ....

57 JEALOUSY BAG

This is thought provoking but good fun! You will need to be sensitive to potential emotions that this exercise may raise to the surface.

Aim: To identify and share things that arouse jealousy and provokes discussion.

YOU WILL NEED

- Post-it notes
- Pens
- An opaque bag

HOW TO DO IT

Ask the group to make a large circle and sit down. Pass around the post-it notes and a pen to each young person. Ask them to write on their piece of paper one thing that makes them feel jealous. You will need to agree some ground rules on this as the slips will be shared later, although they will remain anonymous.

If the group seems slow to start make a few suggestions. This could be something like 'my friend having more CDs than me' or 'my friend being better at football than I am'.

Once everybody has finished, ask him or her to fold the paper so no-one else can see what he or she has written and place it in the bag. Collect the bag and shake it so that the papers get mixed up well. Now pass the bag back around the circle in the opposite direction.

As each person takes the bag they pull out a slip and read the contents. If they pick out their own they should fold it back up and return for someone else.

Leave space for comments or a short discussion after each reading. Are there any duplications or similar themes? Does everyone feel jealous at some stage? Discuss strategies to cope with this emotion.

58 ZIP, ZAP, BOP!

You need at least ten children or young people to make this game work well. Young people usually think that the name is funny and this encourages them to participate.

Aim: This is a team game that needs everybody to work together to keep the imaginary 'hot potato' going round the circle!!

YOU WILL NEED

- A room large enough to make a big circle in

HOW TO DO IT

Ask the children to form a large circle, sitting on the floor. Choose a leader to start the game. The leader pretends he or she is holding a hot potato, and passes it clockwise to the person next to them. As they pass it they say 'ZIP'. You can say 'ZIP' as many times as you wish.

Once this has happened three times the hot potato is allowed to be passed across to the opposite person in the circle. If they choose to do this, they say 'ZAP'. Each participant is only allowed to use a 'ZAP' turn four times in any game.

If a young person does not want the potato passed to them they can say 'BOP'. Each child can only use 'BOP' twice in any game.

If a young person says 'ZAP' when they have used all their 'ZAP' allowances, they lose a 'BOP'. Similarly if a child says 'BOP', having used both turns they lose a 'ZAP'. If you have used all your 'ZAPs' and 'BOPs' you miss a go on the next 'ZIP'.

The game ends when everybody in the group has used all their 'ZAPs' and 'BOPs'!

59 GET KNOTTED!

This team game is really good fun for groups of eight or more. It is a good way to start a session around trust and friendship as team effort is required to be successful!

Aim: This activity encourages young people to start to work together to achieve a group goal.

YOU WILL NEED

- Nothing!

HOW TO DO IT

Ask the group to make a circle, standing next to each other but not so close that they are touching.

Then tell the young people to join hands with two other members of the circle, but not with anyone standing next to them. This is a lot harder than it seems!

Allow about 10 minutes for everyone to be included, making sure that no-one is cheating and everyone is holding onto two other people.

When everybody is in place ask the group to stop, hold the pose and look about them to see what shape the group has formed.

Then set the young people the task of untying themselves and reforming the circle – without breaking hands!

You should end up with the whole group back in a circle, though not necessarily all facing the same way!

60 GROUP FALL

You need to do a risk assessment before you try out this one! Make sure you give clear instructions. If the group is too young or does not really understand what you are asking you could end up with an accident!

Aim: To encourage children to recognise the importance of trust within friendships.

YOU WILL NEED

- Nothing

HOW TO DO IT

Ask the young people to form a circle, including yourself and your co-worker. This will need to be fairly close together with enough space to move quickly to successfully complete the task.

Now ask for a volunteer. Be careful here that the first volunteer is not someone universally unpopular within the group or who is very nervous and unlikely to feel comfortable.

Once you have a volunteer invite them to move to the middle of the circle and ask them to close their eyes.

Explain that the idea of the group fall is to highlight the need for trust within relationships and particularly friends. What you are going to do is to ask the young person in the middle to fall, still with their eyes closed, and as a group you are all going to catch them.

Suggest that if the young people decide to let the volunteer fall, they should consider how they would feel if the same thing happened during their turn.

Review the activity as you go along. How does it feel to have your eyes closed and place your trust in your friends? How does it feel to be responsible for the safety of someone else? What feels more comfortable?

Continue the activity until everybody has experienced both roles.

61 MY SPACE

This is a really good way of introducing the concept of personal space and illustrating that we all have different boundaries and comfort zones.

Aim: To introduce the issue of personal space and body comfort zones.

YOU WILL NEED

- Chalk or a strip of coloured tape

HOW TO DO IT

Divide the group into two equal smaller groups. Draw a chalk line across the half way point in the room. If you have coloured tape stick a strip across the floor in the middle of the room. Try and ensure that this is in a well cleared area so that there are no trip hazards.

Ask Group 1 to stand along the wall facing into the room in a row. Group 2 should now form a straight line along the chalk mark or coloured strip, opposite Group 1.

Ask Group 1 to move slowly towards Group 2, from the opposite side of the area, with their arms outstretched. Group 2 should stand as still as possible.

Members of Group 2 should raise their hands in front of their chests as soon as a young person from Group 1 comes uncomfortably close to them.

Once everyone has done this and all of Group 1 has a partner from Group 2, stop. Ask everyone to stay where they are and look about. The distance or personal space left between each couple will vary depending on what individuals feel comfortable with.

Reflect and discuss this with the group. This can then lead on to work around keeping safe and protective behaviour.

62 THE BUS STOP

This is another drama-based activity designed to encourage young people to engage in role play. It works best with smaller groups of young people who know each other well enough to be confident in arguing their case!

Aim: To enable young people to practice formulating arguments and asserting themselves within a role play environment.

YOU WILL NEED

- Nothing

HOW TO DO IT

Explain to the young people that this activity revolves around a group of strangers waiting to catch a bus.

Ask the group to nominate one person to be the bus driver. This should not be a youth worker as your role will be to facilitate what happens within the group. If you know the group it is an idea to manage this process so that someone can experience the leadership role of bus driver who normally does not get the opportunity.

The rest of the group stands in a line, representing a bus queue. Suggest that they formulate a character for themselves that explains why they are in the bus queue. If they are looking doubtful offer a few ideas yourself – for example, a mother carrying shopping, a man coming home from work, a student on their way back from college.

The bus driver pulls up and says to the queue 'one place, and one place only'.

Each person in the queue then needs to present the reason why they should have the last place on the bus! Encourage the young people to be creative about the reasons they use to tell the bus driver why they need the place. For example, the mother may have children waiting for her at home who will be left alone if she does not get back to relieve the babysitter!

Remind them throughout the process that the final choice lies with the bus driver and only they say who gets the seat.

Once the decision has been made talk the experience through with the group. Did they think it was a good decision? What else could they have said to alter the bus driver's mind? How did it feel to have one person making the decision?

63 THE QUEUE

This activity is really a variation on the bus stop. Once again it encourages young people to formulate arguments and social skills on behalf of themselves.

Aim: To formulate a persuasive argument and express yourself clearly within the group.

YOU WILL NEED

- A set of THE QUEUE cards

HOW TO DO IT

Set the scene by asking the children to form a long line, one in front of the other. Explain that this is now a queue that they are waiting in. You can embellish this if you like. I have set the queue outside a sale of designer labels, waiting for a taxi in the rain or even outside a chip shop!

Once the queue has settled, choose a group member and hand a queue card to them. No-one should see what is on this apart from the person whose turn it is.

The young person with the card then tries to 'jump' the queue by pushing in nearer to the front. They should try and persuade the person they are trying to push in front of to let them in, using the situation on the card as a reason. For example, 'I hope you don't mind me going in front of you but...'

The young person in the queue can then decide if they have been persuaded to let the queue jumper in or not.

Encourage the group to offer opinions on the decision once it has been made – although it cannot be changed! For example, 'Hannah may have said "yes" to you if you were a little less aggressive and explained more...!' or 'that is no excuse for pushing in – ever!'

Once the queue has re-formed select another group member, pass them a card and carry on until everyone has had a go at demonstrating their powers of persuasion!

THE QUEUE

You are a young mother carrying a baby	You are a young wheelchair user
You are a young man carrying a heavy parcel	You are a partially sighted teenager
You are an older woman carrying heavy shopping	You are a business man late for an appointment
You are a doctor and need to get to work	You are a small child who cannot see at the back of the queue
You are an adult wheelchair user	You are a pregnant woman
You are an old man leaning on a walking stick	You are late for school
You are busy and don't have time to queue	You are a pop star and not used to queuing for anything
You are an older person who is not sure if they are in the right queue	You are a young person who has the right money for the goods you want
You are at work and this is your lunch hour	You are an older man who feels faint
You are going to miss your train if you can't jump the queue	You are a teenager and your friend has saved you a place

64 PICTURE SQUARES

This activity illustrates the concept that a successful team is made up of individuals. If it is to work effectively all members of the team need to work together to form a whole.

Aim: To work together to complete a picture. Each young person needs to do their part or the picture will remain incomplete and the task unfinished.

YOU WILL NEED

- A large picture cut into squares – one for each group member
- Large squares of art paper or card – (as many as above)
- The same size piece of mounting card or stiff paper marked out with the squares
- Paint
- Brushes
- Water jars, etc.

HOW TO DO IT

To prepare for the session find a copy of a picture that you think will interest the group. This can be a famous painting, such as Van Gogh's *Sunflowers*, or a photo of a film star or singer. Try and find a picture that is fairly large so that the children can see the detail.

Cut the picture into squares. You will need enough squares for the young people to have one each to study. Put the picture back together and display it on a table so that the children can see what they are aiming for.

When the group arrives show them the picture and ask them to look closely at it. Then take it apart and hand a piece to each child.

Show the group the squares of art paper and explain the task. If you know that they will struggle, suggest they put the puzzle back together onto the mounting board and pencil their name onto the square that they are going to work on. This will stop frustration later.

Allow the group enough time to work on their square. This will depend on how skilled they are at drawing and/or how much the children enjoy art activities. If you know that the answer is 'not much', you could set the task in cartoon form.

Encourage the children to sign their square by weaving their name into the edge of the picture. If this will look silly, you can ask them to sign around the edge of the picture once it is mounted.

Finally, when everything is dry and completed put the squares together with the group to form the picture on the mounting board. Put it on the wall with the original below and review with the group.

A variation of this would be to use a photo of each member of the group to make up the squares. Hand out the photos so that no one is doing himself or herself and mount at the end as a group picture of the children.

ENDINGS

65 POSITIVE THOUGHTS

This evaluation encourages the young people to think about the role that other group members have played in making the session a success for them.

Aim: To encourage the group to identify positive attributes in each other.

YOU WILL NEED

- Nothing

HOW TO DO IT

Ask the group to sit down in a wide circle. Explain that what you would like them to do is to say 'goodbye' and one positive thing to the person on their left and right in the circle. Stress that only positive comments are welcome and make sure no-one is left out or feels isolated. Include yourself and your co-worker in the process.

So, for example, 'Goodbye Donna, I thought you worked really hard in our team game' or 'Goodbye Bradley, thanks for listening to me'.

Finally, go around the circle again and ask the children to say one positive thing about the group itself.

66 TODAY I ...

A quick and easy evaluation method that needs no preparation! It works with any age and size of group.

Aim: To encourage the young people to focus on one positive experience they have had today during the session.

YOU WILL NEED

- Nothing

HOW TO DO IT

Ask the young people to form a circle facing each other. In turn ask them to say 'Today I...' followed by something positive that has happened to them during the session they have just taken part in. This can be factual such as 'Today I met Neelam for the first time', or a response that focuses on feelings such as 'Today I felt confident about standing up for myself'.

If someone is struggling to think of what to say, offer the option to pass and return to him or her at the end of the circle. Make sure no-one feels uncomfortable or pressured into saying something complicated or talk about feelings that have arisen that they don't want to share with the group.

Close the group by offering a 'Today I...' of your own.

67 FACES

A very simple way to get instant feedback of how a session was received by the young people.

Aim: To find out how the group feels after taking part in your session.

YOU WILL NEED

- A post-it note for each group member
- A good range of pens

HOW TO DO IT

Before the session stick a large piece of coloured paper onto the wall. This will become your evaluation board at the end of the activity.

After you have finished the session hand out a post-it note to each young person, with a pen. Ask them to think about how they feel having participated in the session, and then draw a face to represent this on the paper. This should be really simple and show either a smiley, straight or turned down mouth to represent how they feel.

When they have drawn their face ask them to stick the note onto the piece of coloured paper on the wall. Ask the young people to look at all the stickers. Are there mainly happy or sad faces?

Collect them in and use as part of your evaluation for the session.

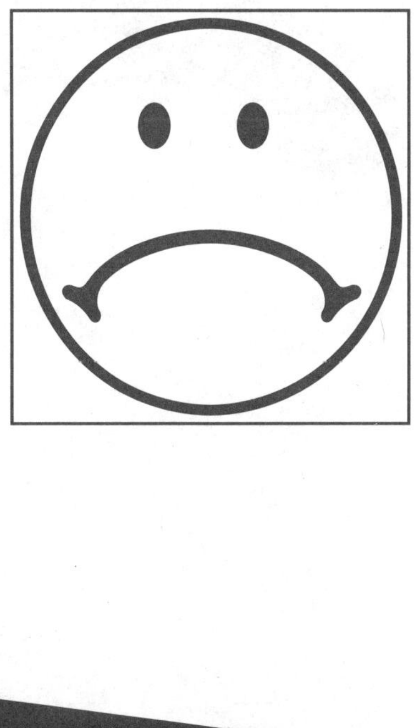

68 CIRCLE TIME

Circles are good ways to end sessions so that everyone can see each other and nobody feels outside the group.

Aim: To get feedback from each member of the group without interruption from the others.

YOU WILL NEED

- Any small object that can be passed around the group

HOW TO DO IT

Ask the group to form a circle with the youth workers. Show the children the object you have chosen. This could be something like a pen, but you could choose something with more significance. I have used a small teddy or a ball.

Explain that only the person holding the object can speak. When they have finished they pass it onto the next member of the group.

Ask questions that will evaluate the session. For example, 'What part of this activity did you enjoy most?' 'Tell me one thing you learnt.' Make sure you ask the same question of each person to get an overall picture. The number of questions you ask will depend on the size of the group.

Review the answers after the session with your co-worker and record the findings.

69 PICTURE THIS...

This is another drama-based technique for evaluating how young people feel about the experiences they have just shared. It is suitable for groups of all ages and ability.

Aim: To use a visualisation process to enable young people to assess their own feelings and learning.

YOU WILL NEED

- Candles and matches (optional)
- Music (optional)

HOW TO DO IT

How you create a relaxed, calm environment is up to you and the area you have to work in. One suggestion is to light candles, dim the lights and play music quietly in the background. I have used New Age tapes of the sea and sea creatures to provide a tranquil setting to encourage the young people to relax.

Once you have set the scene ask the children to either sit or lie down quietly with their eyes closed. You can use some basic relaxation techniques to focus the group, such as flexing and relaxing limbs and breathing deeply.

As the group begins to chill out ask that they picture a swimming pool on a warm, sunny day in their head. Describe the pool in detail, including a deep end with a diving board and a shallow end with steps out. You can be as creative as you want.

Now, suggest that each person uses the image of the swimming pool in their head to represent the session they have just taken part in. Where do they see themselves? Struggling in the deep end? Somewhere in the middle? Watching from the side or desperate to dive in? If visualisation is a new experience for the young people use some of these suggestions to get the group thinking of their own. Encourage the sharing of ideas.

Finally, close the session by telling the group to relax and open their eyes gradually as you count to 20.

70 EVALUATION LETTER

This evaluation sheet asks for a personal view of the session that the child has just participated in. It is easy to complete as it is devised as a letter pro-forma. The young person just has to fill in the gaps!

Aim: To encourage young people to offer feedback and reflect on an experience.

YOU WILL NEED

- Copies of the EVALUATION LETTER
- Pens

HOW TO DO IT

Hand out copies of the sheet and read it through as a whole group to make sure that everyone understands what is in the letter. Ask young people to look at their own copy and think about the gaps it contains.

Ask them to reflect on the session they have just experienced and fill in the spaces with their thoughts and opinions.

Depending on how well you know the group and the level of confidence the young people have, encourage the group to share their responses.

If you do not think that this would be appropriate you can discuss them individually or collect in and review later. Similarly the letters can remain anonymous if you think that this will get more honest feedback.

EVALUATION LETTER

Date

Dear Worker,

The bit I enjoyed most about this session was . . . .

If we did it again . . . . *would make it*

even better.

I learnt . . . . *from the activities*

about myself, and . . . . *about other*

members of the group.

Before next time the goals I have set myself are . . . .

. . . . *which we can talk about then.*

See you soon

From

. . . .

71 HEADLINES

This is a group evaluation that produces a joint piece of work that depicts the collective experience. As it takes time you may want to use this during the final session of a project. You can use it with groups of up to six young people.

Aim: To produce a newspaper front page that shows the group experience of the project they have just taken part in.

YOU WILL NEED

- Newspapers and magazines
- Scissors
- Glue
- Large sheets of paper
- Marker pens

HOW TO DO IT

Hand out paper, glue, scissors and markers to each group of four to six young people. Make available a good selection of magazines and newspapers.

Explain to the children that the task is to create a newspaper front page to show what has been learnt/experienced during the project they have been working on.

Suggest that the young people use both marker pens and cut out letters from the newspapers to make the headlines and then devise their copy to go with it. This should include how they feel, what they liked best and anything the groups would like followed up in a further session.

Once the front pages are complete display them on the wall and invite the young people to review each other's, asking questions or explaining sections as they go along. You can then leave it up as a record of the event for other club members to see.

72 GIFTS

This evaluation encourages the young people to recognise positive aspects in each other and 'give' it as a gift at the end of the session.

Aim: To promote support and positive regard for group members and raise self-esteem.

YOU WILL NEED

- Small pieces of paper
- Pens
- Bag

HOW TO DO IT

Hand out pieces of paper to each group member. If you have a small group give a piece of paper for each member, if you have a large number of young people hand out one piece only.

Explain that you would like them to write an individual message on their paper for each person in the group. Stress that this should be positive, but should include something relating to the session. For example, 'Ruben – thanks for making me laugh' or 'Siobhan – you always listen to everyone's ideas'.

Ask the young people to fold their message unsigned, and write the name of the person they intend to receive the 'gift' on the front.

Collect the gifts and place in the bag. Give it a good shake and then walk among the group distributing the slips of paper. Depending on the young people, they can either look at their gifts within the group or take them away with them to read later.

Each member of the group should now have some positive feedback about their contribution to the group process.